I0439037

This text has been provided by the author in limited quantities strictly for the designated readership. Future reproductions may be purchased through On-Demand Publishing, LLC located at CreateSpace.com, through Amazon.com, Barnes & Noble, and other book distributors.

Copyright © 2014 by Brendan Zottl
All rights reserved.

Published and distributed by On-Demand Publishing, LLC with provisional permission granted by the author, Brendan Zottl

On-Demand Publishing, Inc
100 Enterprise Way, Suite A200
Scotts Valley, CA 95066

No part of this publication (ISBN 978-1495498046) may be reproduced, stored in a retrieval system, or transmitted in any form or by any means; electronic, mechanical, photocopying, recording, scanning, or otherwise, except when permitted under Section 107 or 108 of the 1976 United States Copyright Act, without written authorization of the author - Brendan Zottl.

Cover design by Brendan Zottl and TLC Multimedia Inc.

Printed in the United States of America.
First Trade Printing: March 2014

10 9 8 7 6 5 4 3 2 1

Limit of Liability & Disclaimer of Legal and Civil Responsibility

This publication is strictly intended for educational and informational purposes and should not be solely relied on for planning. The advice and strategies contained herein may not be suitable for individual situations and the author makes no guarantee that the data provided is accurate. The information contained in this publication does not take the place of licensed, legal professionals. This text is provided "as-is," and the reader assumes all responsibility for any decisions made as a result of information provided within these pages. This book is not meant to instruct the reader on any particular scenario. The reader shall also assume that the information provided by this publication is no more accurate than may be obtained elsewhere, and the author is thus not responsible for any implications or actions taken by the reader.

PROPER RV SELECTION

Recreational vehicle buyers have a myriad of choices in today's competitive marketplace. This book will make buying decisions more streamlined and assist readers as they locate, negotiate, and buy the perfect RV. People purchase a recreational vehicle because they want to be able to do what they want, when they want to do so. It has always been difficult to combine one's love for travel with an actual fixed dwelling. Traveling in a RV is like owning a vacation home in every area that a family would ever want to visit. Combing those two attributes with a wide open itinerary allows individuals complete freedom that is theirs for the taking! Imagine camping by a babbling brook or a panoramic hilltop vista while still being able to enjoy all the modern conveniences of the 21st century. With a motorcoach everyone can easily do so!

With the proper RV, one is able to walk alongside a mountain trail in the morning, come back for a hot lunch and shower all before settling down and enjoying the sports game in the afternoon. After the game, step outside again and take pleasure in an evening of fishing or hunting before walking back and retiring to a full nights rest in a comfortable bed! Everyone traveling has his or her own belongings, place to sleep, and one of the most comfortable modes of travel.

There are numerous benefits to buying a recreational vehicle. Of course, there is an upfront cost of purchase. But once it's been fully paid, aside from small monthly bills to top off the tanks with fuel and for scheduled maintenance, it is essentially rent-free living for as long as the owner stays in the vehicle. This is much more economical than renting a vacation house for a week or staying in a hotel for just as long. Nearly all RVs have full kitchens, a comfortable bedroom, couch and chairs within the living space, and even an area for a mobile office or whatever other special concerns their owners have.

After buying a recreational vehicle there are over twelve thousand campgrounds, parks, and popular tourist attractions to visit in North America alone. These happen along interstates, in cities, and throughout small and medium sized towns according to the Recreation Vehicle Industry Association (RVIA). Essentially, anywhere there can be a campground, there likely is. The trick is finding a spot that matches the owners' wants and needs during the time they want to stay. Using the internet to find both public and private campgrounds makes RVing a breeze. Other great resources are travel guides, magazines, campground directories, and state tourism boards to consult when planning a RV trip.

Before setting off on a journey of a lifetime, one just needs to buy a recreational vehicle. This book serves to help people find the right vehicle to suit their needs without overpaying for the purchase.

A recreational vehicle is a means of transportation that combines a living and bathing quarters that are suitable for the purposes of entertaining, leisure, sleeping, and everyday life. Recreational vehicles debuted a century ago, but those "auto-campers" were nothing like today's luxurious models. Original RVs came with chamber pots, low ceilings, and single burner gas stoves. Modern RVs come with nearly every convenience of a modern home and then some! These features and the ease of use have contributed to almost nine million American households that enjoy RVing every year!

Recreational Vehicles are described as a "home on wheels", and that is a great description. These rigs are "self contained" meaning that the RV travels around fully capable of operating on its own accord. It does not need to be hooked up (like a conventional house) to water lines, a sewer system, the electric grid, gas lines, and the like. Composting or holding tanks will maintain waste until their owners have a chance to dump it in a suitable dumping station or sewer.

It's important to note that this is a book about recreational vehicles as opposed to fixed manufactured housing units. The latter are towed to their destination by a hired truck and available in either single, double, or triple-wide configuration. These are installed semi-permanently within a trailer park or on a plot of land and are about as agile as an anvil. The two lifestyles are as different as night and day and there is very little overlap between the folks who purchase one or the other.

Prices for new RVs vary widely and can range from ten thousand dollars when purchasing the smallest folding camping trailer to over a million dollars, or more, when purchasing the most luxurious coach conversion with just about every price point in between. Selecting the proper RV is of utmost importance to the happiness of the end user. Whether spending a weekend in the community park or traveling across the country to live in the desert for months, not only will this be an individual or family home on wheels for the length of their travels, but it's important that everyone feels comfortable and secure. Make sure that everyone will be able to stand the company of everyone else who will be traveling along and that there is ample room for storage of their belongings. Having room for daily necessities including clothes, shoes, toiletries, and the like is crucial to their level of satisfaction and overall enjoyment.

There are two main categories of RVs. There are motorhomes that come with an attached engine and towables which do not. To travel, the latter are towed behind the family car, truck, van, or even another motorhome.

A RV is a fully self contained mobile dwelling, equipped with running water, toilet, sleeping areas, and a kitchen with amenities such as a microwave, stove, refrigerator, air conditioning, and much more. There are several types from which to choose. Motorized RVs include the following types; bus conversions, types A, B, and C, toy haulers, and truck or van conversions. Type A motorhomes and bus conversions are generally the largest. Type B motorhomes and van campers are the smallest; and Type C motorhomes, truck conversions, and toy haulers generally fall in between though modern class C's may be just as large as class A's depending on their body and chassis configuration as well as their height and length.

Types of towable RVs include camping trailers, expandable trailers, truck campers, conventional travel trailers, fifth-wheel trailers, and the least common, known as a Sports Utility RV (also sometimes referred to as a toy hauler).

The main advantages of bus conversion motorhomes are found in their build, durability, potential for luxury appointments and an extremely powerful drive-train. These vehicles are built to last from

the base of the undercarriage to the top of the roofline. They generally outlast any other type of RV by hundreds of thousands, if not millions of road miles! They can withstand nearly all rough road and weather conditions while still

being easy to handle and drive. Although they are huge vehicles, the suspension has been tuned to make them surprisingly agile as they cruise down the highway. If modern features and luxury appointments are important and cost is not of concern, this is probably the ideal motorhome to buy. It's akin to a luxury condominium on wheels. Many feature what is referred to as a "slide out" or "pop out". This is a feature which provides for extra living space that is created as the walls of the RV extend outward from the interior while parked. Modern motorhomes typically have at least one slide and there are models that feature up to five.

The engines used for bus conversions are among the most powerful and there will never be problems passing other vehicles on the highway or rural road. Even climbing the steepest mountain grades isn't an issue with such an ample power train. The powerful engines make it a breeze to tow boats, cars, or other vehicles behind a bus conversion. It's comforting to know that when stepping on the accelerator, the power will always be there to accomplish whatever the driver needs.

The primary disadvantages of these recreational vehicles are their expansive length and width as well as the initial cost of acquisition, and their ongoing maintenance and repair costs. Although they can be the most durable of RVs, they can be hard to maneuver in urban and suburban areas and are the most complex and expensive to repair, by a significant amount. It's important to note that the work cannot be completed by the local auto or truck shop. This means that owners will have to drop them off at a suitable facility that specializes in bus maintenance and repair. Just buying a bus conversion does not end the investment. Although they last much longer between scheduled maintenance when compared with other RV types, their owners should be sure to factor in plenty of money for their necessary maintenance and repair when they are in the shop. A major drive-train issue may run into the thousands or even tens of thousands of dollars.

However, coach conversions are built to last and will typically run for a million miles, or more before encountering any major issues with the chassis, drive-train, or motor. They come in a wide variety of sizes and types and sleep between two and 14 people! Models that sleep over six people are typically configured in an arrangement called a bunkhouse where multiple beds are stacked atop one another in the center of the vehicle (like the bunks for enlisted men on a naval ship). These motorhomes start at $40,000 for the most basic used conversions with very high mileage and run up into the high end where brand new luxurious models can easily exceed one million dollars.

Living space inside a bus conversion or class A may rival that of a one bedroom condominium and the amenities may even be much more comprehensive and luxurious. This brings us to type A recreational vehicles which are nearly tied for the roomiest of RVs, along with bus conversions.

They feature among the most interior and storage space, but at a much more reasonable cost than a brand new bus conversion. When most folks hear the word motorhome, they usually envision a class A. These motorhomes are usually built on a specific chassis, such those manufactured by Ford, Freightliner, Spartan and others. The living area of this coach is built on top of this chassis, with the engine being mounted to the chassis itself. Engines include front, mid-coach, or rear designs and everything from very small six cylinders to 12 cylinder truck engines.

Class A motorhomes are among the most popular, largest, self-contained, and full featured motorhomes available. Typically class A motorhomes are shaped more like a box leading to their

decreased curb appeal, but just as much interior room and available storage space when compared with a bus conversion. The downside to all this space is the loss of aerodynamics and fuel efficiency over many other types of motorhome. These RVs come

in a wide variety of shapes and sizes and in a typical configuration, have a sleeping capacity between three and eight people. Amenities include a kitchen, sleeping area, one or two bathrooms, entertainment systems, dining facilities and up to four slideouts. Modern living systems include electricity, heating, air conditioning, water, and propane gas. The newest models feature an all electric option which negates the need for natural gas and uses electric cooktops instead of gas burners. Some RVers have even elected to forgo generators and recharge their house batteries using renewable energy such as solar and wind. More luxurious models include multiple flat screen TVs, an exterior grill and refrigerator (typically stationed in one of the basement bays), satellite TV, high speed wireless internet, and much more. Prices range from $55,000 to over a half a million dollars when they are sold in new condition.

The most expensive tend to have the look of a better equipped bus and typically come with a rear diesel engine (known as a pusher). Class A motorhomes are manufactured by an array of companies and the configurations are nearly endless. Consumers will find that all of these motorhomes are built upon a chassis that was originally designed for use as a large truck or people mover.

RVs of the class A variety are somewhat more challenging to drive on small roads, but just as easy as most other types while cruising down the highway. They are more suitable to novice RVers than bus conversions because they do not have as expansive of a cockpit monitoring center. They usually have fewer controls and the ones that are available are more user-friendly because the manufacturer knows that they will typically not be driven by those with a commercial driver's license, unlike many buses which are driven by professionals.

Class A's offer some of the most generous storage options as many come with a RV basements that looks much like the luggage compartments at the base of buses. Typically they are configured with at least eight slideout bays that have locking doors. These bays are a great area for storing all the necessities that families or fulltimers bring along with them.

When folks in a class A arrive at their destination, there is no need to get out of the RV during times of inclement weather. The options on some models are quite literally endless. There are entertainment systems, lighting, custom cabinets, flooring, and much more to choose from. Just about all models come with a pair of captain's chairs towards the front of the coach that is used for driving and then swivel around when parked to become an integral part of the living area.

When towing a motorhome, as opposed to arriving in a coach propelled by its own motor, there is a certain amount of campground setup that has to be done. Initially, the towable needs to be unhooked and everyone inside will physically need to transfer themselves and their belongings from the tow vehicle to the RV to actually begin to get comfortable. With a Class A, among other motorhomes, everyone is already home wherever they park. Not only that, they usually arrive more relaxed and in comfort and style knowing that they do not have as much work as those rigs that require extensive campground setup.

Disadvantages include a generally more expensive acquisition price than all other RVs (except bus conversions), their length and width may make it more cumbersome to drive than most other vehicles. Additionally, their repair costs are usually more than smaller RVs since there are fewer repair shops that are able to handle their expansive length and girth. Unfortunately, Class A motorhomes are usually very expensive and as more manufacturers keep packing in expensive features that trend will only grow even more so. New units also take the most serious depreciation hit, as they are among the most common. Buyers should bear that in mind before purchasing.

Additionally, if drivers intend to get around town once they arrive at their destination, they will probably need to tow another vehicle behind the coach, adding to the overall cost of the total arrangement. It's just too difficult to set up camp and subsequently pull-in the slideouts and take down the awnings every time their owners want to jaunt to the store. Of course, sometimes owners opt for bicycles of motorbikes, but these may limit not only how far one may travel, but they are much less useable during times of inclement weather.

If the motorhome breaks down, its owners will probably have to spend a night or two in a hotel while it is at the RV repair shop. This is as opposed to motorhomes that are towed where the owners still maintain their mobile residence. The good thing is that they will sleep soundly knowing at least the repairs will be much cheaper than those owners cruising down the road in a bus conversion. Most shops try to have vehicles repaired and back out on the road that same day, but if the repair is serious enough, or parts are hard to acquire, that just may not be possible. With a towed vehicle, owners still have their home to stay in if the tow vehicle has to be serviced for an extended period of time.

Class A RVs can be very long, which is great for those looking for the most interior space. This is especially true for the more expensive models, but that can narrow the number of campsites where their owners may stay. Some campgrounds simply don't have the facilities to accommodate the longest and widest rigs.

On the opposite side of the size spectrum are type B recreational vehicles. These are commonly referred to as van campers, though not all reside on a van chassis. These drive just as easily as the family van, albeit with a greater height clearance, and they sleep between two and four people with up to two slideouts. These motorhomes will be quite familiar in terms of handling and gas mileage to a conventional SUV or truck. Because of its small size, this motorhome can continue to be used as a family car around town which is one of the major selling points. Prices range from just over $40,000 to well over a hundred thousand dollars when purchased in new condition.

Class B vehicles are usually built with a high top added so that standing up inside is possible. They are very easy to drive and may be parked virtually anywhere making these RVs very popular. Unlike

 most other motorized RVs, class B vehicles typically only have only four tires. They can be serviced by the owner or virtually any car dealership or repair shop. The space is significantly tighter inside, but feature most of the same amenities found in larger RVs. Often a class B is as expensive as or even more so than a class C motorhome, as they have to be carefully hand built and fitted and this takes longer in such a small space.

Their construction typically begins with a chassis and frame manufactured by an automaker that is modified in appearance for transportation and recreation by a company specializing in customized vehicles. Changes may include the installation of a full-size side or rear entry door, larger windows, more plush carpeting, extra insulation paneling, custom seats, sofas, and assorted accessories such as upgraded carbon fiber or wood control panel and a sunroof. Most class B conversions provide comfortable seating for between five and seven folks, though some seat as many as a dozen passengers. Models typically feature a small microwave and mini-fridge as well as enough counter space to prepare a light meal like a breakfast comprised of eggs and bacon or a lunch of salad and sandwiches. Because of their limited space, this would probably not be the right vehicle for those who enjoy cooking, entertaining, or a combination of both. Most class B RVs also do not have full time sleeping arrangements. So, buyers who dislike the idea of a pullout couch or Murphy bed may want to look for other RV alternatives.

One of the most positive aspects of a class B is that it is more aerodynamic than other RV types and as such goes much farther than other rigs on the same amount of fuel. Many manufacturers report over 20 miles per gallon with the most lightweight of the class achieving up to 25 mpg!

For those folks who intend to constantly garage their motorhome, leave it parked in a driveway or yard, or even stealthily camp off the grid in an urban or suburban environment, even on occasion, these may be the ideal class for them. They are the most streamlined motorhomes and typically even conform to home owner's association guidelines. This is because their air conditioners and satellite dishes are typically built into the roofline or hidden behind paneling and not visible from the roadway.

Manufacturers are beginning to make class B recreational vehicles more luxurious than ever before and some even feature multiple slideouts! Buyers now have leather chairs and couches, various options for carbon fiber, stainless steel, wood trim, and up to three flat screen televisions! Coach builders are becoming more innovative and have developed products that have Murphy beds which recline into the walls, tables and chairs that turn into beds, integrated window screens set between panels of glass,  televisions that popup from countertops or integrated into the furniture, and even electronics that reside inside the ceiling or within cabinetry when not in use.

A sub-segment of the type B recreational vehicle is the pickup or sport utility vehicle (SUV) conversion. This is where a truck or multipurpose vehicle is produced in the aftermarket by an alerter or final stage manufacturer. It may contain modifications to which at least one Federal Motor Vehicle Safety Standard is applicable and is designed for the transportation of people for recreation, traveling more comfortably off-road, or extended length road travel. For instance, many limousine companies buy vehicles of this type and offer them to corporate executives so they are able to comfortably work during their rush hour commutes, to or from the airport, or even while they are being shuttled between cities. As traveling by air or train has become more restrictive and more crowded, these vehicle types have skyrocked in popularity.

The detractions of class B vehicles is that their interior storage and passenger space is more limited, typically all cooking is done via hotplate or microwave as there is not enough space for an oven or conventional rangetop. Along those lines, typically there is not enough space inside for more than two people to be comfortable. In addition, to use the bed often times, the couch or chairs must be folded away, leaving no room to sit or lay down other than the space reserved for sleeping. Many people find this too cumbersome for conventional relaxation. If either the husband or wife is a early riser and the other likes to stay up late, class B layouts may be overly cumbersome.

On the flip side, they get much better gas mileage than larger coaches and since their length is typically only around 20 feet, they often fit into conventional parking spaces, and make tight turns which the vast majority of other RV types are unable.

If someone decides they need more space and storage room than a class B provides, but do not need all of amenities or floorspace of a class A or bus conversion than a class C may be right for them. A class C, also called a mini-motorhome has similar amenities to a type A's but in a smaller, more

mobile, and easier to maneuver package. It is as if a Class A and Class B motorhome made love and created this vehicle as their offspring. Class C RVs are hybrid motorhomes that tend to bring several of the benefits of both classes and combine them into a vehicle of medium size. Typically, these RVs are built larger than a type B and are among the most versatile of RV categories that feature up to three slideouts. With an optional space over the cab that is converted into either an entertainment center, storage space, or sleeping area, these RVs comfortably sleep between four and eight folks. They range in price from $48,000 to over $300,000 in new condition. The latter price point is for those built on professional truck chassis and with the largest, most durable engines. Most class C RVs feature four wheels in the rear of the vehicle to handle the additional weight and stress to the frame.

The feature that gets the most attention is the sleeping area that is built over the cab. Ironically, many people just use it for storage, a place for their pets, or an entertainment system area. Class C motorhomes have typically been built with gasoline engines, but are more frequently being offered with diesels as people realize the cost to benefit ratio is more in their favor with a diesel drive-

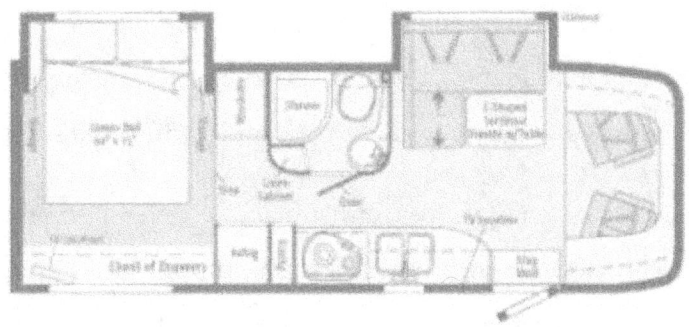

train. Customarily, they have been built on either a GM or Ford chassis but some manufacturers have started using European chassis, such as those by Mercedes. The benefits to these vehicles are that they secure better gas mileage and torque than their gasoline counterparts. Some RVs are even being built atop a big rig chassis which make them look much different than their smaller class companions. Typically these cater to the luxury RV and performance oriented crowd and are known as a super class C rig. Because of their big-rig strength, they are among the best haulers available and will easily handle the largest loads with ease. They vary in length from under 20ft to over 40ft. The longer variations rival class A vehicles in terms of interior space, usability, and storage capacity. Newer class C's also incorporate multiple slide outs which allows for more interior room while parked. In general, the class C motorhome tends to be tighter on space than a class A but have much more than the class B. The space over the cab is often ideal for families who need to maximize sleeping arrangements. Many of the rigs in this class will drive much like larger SUVs. Except for when ascending the steepest hills, modern class C vehicles drive almost effortlessly.

A super C is comprised of a heavy duty truck chassis, engine, and transmission with living quarters and up to two bathrooms that are affixed behind the cab. Essentially, it is a class C motorhome on 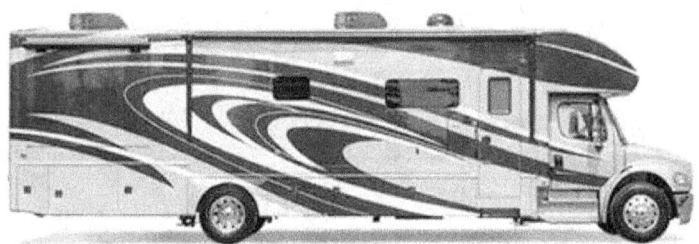 steroids! It features a large diesel engine (such as is most common in a big-rig 18 wheeler, also known as a "lorry" throughout Europe), a heavy duty transmission, and a reinforced chassis to handle the extra stress and weight. It is designed to travel millions of miles without failure and it is usually set up for heavy duty towing. Most of the folks who purchase these larger vehicles intend on bringing along their boat, car, ATVs, or even towing another RV behind them! These trucks are typically configured in such a manner and built for the trucking industry before being converted for use as a recreational vehicle. A trucking company will typically drive 200,000 miles per year and these heavy duty vehicles are meant to withstand such rigorous duty.

Dynamax and Jayco each manufacture several popular models in this category and these RVs have many benefits over other classes of motorhome. They include that the truck chassis is very easy to repair and service. Simply pop the hood and the mechanic has easy access to the motor. This means that no longer will a greasy mechanic be traipsing through the interior, and even the bedroom to service the drive-train or motor. These units drive very comfortably once underway, even though they are of considerable size. Most RVers report that they do not feel significantly different than driving the truck cab by itself because of the ample power. The motorhome section follows along as if it does not weigh anything at all. Plus, just like in smaller class C's the cab features driver and co-pilot doors for easy entry and exit. These rigs are also known to be safer than almost any other RV type. This is because they have a low center of gravity due to their weight. In addition, in the event of a head-on collision, the front of the cab is designed to absorb impact. Due to the vehicle's considerable size and weight, drivers are  also much less likely to be injured. It is overall a much safer design than typical diesel pushers or other RVs that are of the same length, weight, and width. Because of their heavy duty engineering and design, like other diesel engines, they will run for many miles before needing to be serviced.

However, on the downside, super C motorhomes cost much more than just about any other type of RV, except for bus conversions and the highest end of luxury class A's. They are typically much larger and wider as well which makes them more difficult to maneuver within tight campsites and on smaller roads. They can run well over 40 feet in length and if filled with luxury amenities and the newest electronics may easily cost upwards of half a million dollars! Typically, that cost prices them out of reach for individuals that would normally purchase a class C recreational vehicle. They also get among the worst gas mileage of any recreational vehicle, at well under ten miles per gallon.

The next set of RVs is known as towable trailers. These are units with a living space that is towed by another vehicle. These trailers range from the lightest pop-outs to the heaviest fifth-wheel trailers and almost anything in between. Although towable trailers usually have floor plans that are more kid-friendly and family oriented --- e.g., they offer multiple bedrooms and more seating than those in motorhomes, which are usually targeted to couples, there are many luxurious travel trailers and fifth-wheels on the market. Towable trailers have a number of advantages over their motorized home counterparts, mainly that they easier to store when not in use. This quality is especially helpful for owners who only use their RVs a few months a year. Most folks only camp during the warm months and having a trailer that can be easily parked is advantageous.

Living in a towable trailer feels more like living in a conventional house than does a motorized RV that is pulled, or pushed by an engine. The actual living space in a towable trailer is 100 percent of the total interior area whereas, the motorhome, on the other hand, requires space dedicated to the driving area --- e.g., the steering wheel, dashboard, driver and passenger seats, and windshield. People may feel that sleeping in a towable trailer feels more like sleeping in a bedroom than sleeping in a motorhome, which may feel like sleeping aboard a bus or van.

Once at the chosen destination, the towing vehicle can be separated from the trailer and used as transportation around the area. This is especially advantageous when the recreational vehicle stays at one campsite for an extended amount of time or when the campsite is particularly far from area attractions, entertainment, grocery stores, or gas stations.

Because a towable trailer doesn't have an engine, it has no extra motor upkeep while it remains parked. Motorhomes, on the other hand, have engines that require maintenance even when they're not being used. Motorhome owners also may tow a small car, which not only adds to the motorhome's fuel consumption but again requires maintenance on yet another vehicle. If the towing vehicle breaks down and requires extensive repairs, these RVers can still live in the towable trailer at the campsite until the repairs are completed. Staying in a motel or hotel can get expensive, especially for large families. This is a cost that those in towable do not have to bear.

A towable trailer has a wide range of towing vehicles that can pull it, including a six-cylinder or larger motor. This includes many sedans, SUVs, minivans, and pickup trucks, so the vehicle can be chosen that best fits the trip. The lightest weight units may even be towed by four cylinder vehicles. If a family is planning its vacation at a resort, for example, a sedan may be the better choice. If camping in the backwoods or far from paved roads, a pickup truck may be a better tow vehicle.

One of the largest advantages of towables is that they may be towed behind another RV. If the towable trailer is hooked up to a smaller truck camper, a truck with a camper top or a van conversion, then two RVs are available while camping. One can serve as base camp and the other can be used for off-road excursions, or one can be used for parents and the other for the in-laws, friends, or kids. Another benefit is that it is always easier to trade in an individual trailer or tow vehicle separately than it is to sell the whole setup when upgrading. Trading an all-in-one motorhome usually takes much longer because it is a more expensive purchase to begin with and the systems are much more complicated than trailers themselves which do not have an engine or as extensive electronics setup. Along these lines, finding a motorhome retail establishment that is willing to pay what the owner thinks the rig is worth is more difficult. Many places will take trailers and other towables, but will not accept motorized class A, bus conversions, and the like as they are more difficult to sell RVs. Towables are also easier for individuals to sell as a private party. This is because buyers are not as concerned with the more complicated systems that are more prevalent in larger RVs as focus primarily on aesthetics and construction. Consequently, the time and energy spent by an individual will likely be less than when selling a larger RV. Taking into account all the time and energy spent, plus money for advertising and more, selling a motorhome can be a much more daunting prospect than selling a towable.

Folding camping trailers (also known as pop-ups or pop-downs) are lightweight units with partially collapsible sides that fold for more aerodynamic towing by a motorized vehicle. It has the added benefit of easy storage when collapsed in a garage or carport. The smallest units may even be towed by compact cars or larger motorbikes (such as touring models). Though similar in set up to a large tent, they are much more durable and provide kitchen, dining, and sleeping facilities for up to eight people.

They are remarkably easy to tow when compared with to travel trailer and fifth wheel models. Pop-ups also are the easiest to park within the towing categories. Once arriving at a destination, the

pop-up camper transforms into an extravagant tent with a rigid skeleton in mere minutes. It offers a multiple beds as well as up to two showers (one inside and one outside), and an optional conventional toilet. They come in lengths from eight feet (when folded) to a maximum of 30 feet (unfolded). They also have an interior height of up to eight feet depending on the model. These units make a great all purpose motorhome. However, these motorhomes are primarily designed for small overnight or weekend trips. If spending a lot of time in an RV is important to the purchaser, this may not the best choice.

The most luxurious models feature high side walls that move up and down electronically, and heavy-duty insulation to maintain the heating and air conditioning levels. If the consumer is willing to spend their money on available upgrades they will find up to three slideouts, multiple television sets, a small gas range or electric stovetop, small refrigerator such as in a studio apartment, and even a bathroom with an optional standup shower! Some even feature room separators, collapsible closets, tiny outdoor grills, and sinks that function just like small kitchens! Models can comfortably sleep several couples or a large family and range from six thousand dollars to $30,000 in new condition. Forest River and Jayco manufacture dozens of different models with literally hundreds of options and these RVs have made huge strides in a class once known for being just simple tents on wheels!

A subset of the pop-up trailer category is the "A-frame" known for having hard walls on all sides in a triangle-shaped configuration. These are newer, more innovative designs that allow for better climate control, and in some cases, an even quicker setup than more conventional RVs in this same category. With practice, or automatic motors, some models are able to be fully setup in less than 30 seconds!

An A-frame camper is perfect for those folks who like the idea of a hard-sided travel trailer that is lightweight and very easy to tow. All of these models fold down into an almost flat configuration, just like a tent trailers but these lift up to a small cabin-style camper. Due to the styling of an A-shaped roofline, the headroom is very low towards the sides and taller individuals may have a hard time enjoying the time spent inside. Towing an A-frame is easy on most vehicles and will only reduce gas mileage by about five miles per gallon. This negligible fuel mileage differential makes them an attractive option for those with greater financial constraints. A-frame trailers sleep far less people and have less interior room than comparably sized tent trailers and this has made them a tough sell popular in the marketplace. Most of the models for sale only sleep two people through some floor plans may sleep up to four people with an optional folding dinette table that turns into another sleeping area. Towing an A-frame trailer is almost as easy as towing a tent trailer, but they weight slightly more because of their hard size and additional latches. They are almost unaffected by strong winds while being towed and once setup at the campsite. This is a major benefit over their popup counterparts. Plus, since they also fold down, it's easy to see out the rearview and side mirrors while driving, unlike larger towables. Since these towables are much more unique than their tent-style counterparts, they are relegated to the back of campgrounds much less often, and occasionally are even placed near the premium spots next to teardrop RVs. Unfortunately, due to their space limitations and insulation limitations, these RVs are still generally not considered suitable for full time camping. Though, they do make for great family fun during the warmer spring and summer months!

Another class of RV, the truck camper, is unique in that it features a separate unit that is loaded onto or affixed to the bed and / or chassis of a pickup truck. Many have kitchen and permanent bathroom facilities and up to three slideouts. The interior room is typically comparable to a class B, albeit with a much more limited storage capacity.

Truck campers have come a long way in a very short amount of time. In the past decade, there are more luxurious models than ever and towards the upper end of the truck camper market, there are even units that feature separate bedroom, kitchen, and living rooms! This would have been unheard of just a decade ago, and some models are almost as large inside as the smaller class C vehicles. However, on the downside, these truck campers typically only fit the beds of, and are able to be

hauled by, the largest trucks with a capacity of at least two tons or greater. Some of the larger models also require a bed length of greater than 12 feet. These are typically referred to as "long-bed" trucks and as some of these RV models are over 20 feet in total length, only the largest truck beds will fit these requirements.

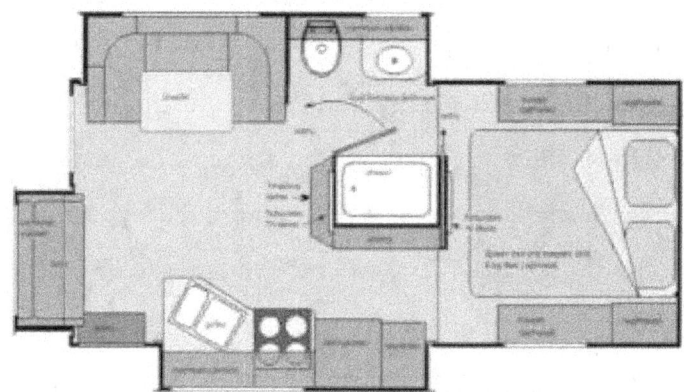

Truck campers most often sleep two to four people, though some models even sleep six adults! They are most typically configured with a bed over the cab area and at least one couch towards the rear. They sell from between $8,000 for the most basic model that is not much more than a tent atop a truck bed and up to $55,000 for the largest models in new condition with up to three slideouts. Newer models feature options including a satellite dish and solar panels that are installed at or before the time of purchase.

Truck campers have been designed with the resourceful in mind. If a pickup truck is already owned, than this may be the perfect RV solution. This type of RV is available for a fraction of the price of a motorhome and owners will find that they may add most of the RV features to the back of their pickup truck. The camper is fairly simple to remove should access to the truck bed be necessary. Those who gravitate towards boondocking in the wild are especially apt to purchase these RVs because they are the least limited when traveling on rough or uneven terrain or on steep grades. Other RVs simply cannot go where truck camper are able. Plus, most of the newer models come with the vast majority of creature comforts that other RVs feature so truck campers are less of a compromise than ever before!

Truck manufacturers provide their consumers with specific ratings to help determine the capacities of the engine, drive train, chassis, and towing ability. It is of utmost importance for RVers to follow these mandates as failure to do so may cause major issues. Most of these ratings are posted on the driver's side door jam, on a label inside the glove box, within the owner's manual, or amongst other literature. If a truck is already owned that is intended to be used as a camper, it's always wise to take the vehicle to a commercial truck scale to determine the actual weight of the truck. That information along with truck capacity information will help determine the remaining capacities for carrying and towing. Camper weights both dry and wet vary depending on what optional equipment that is installed and how full the holding tanks are. Also, take into consideration the weight of the passengers, their gear, and trailer tongue weight (if applicable). Truck and camper package handling can be greatly improved by the addition of support equipment like air springs, special shocks absorbers, and cabover shocks. Because this class of RV has only one set of brakes, it's incredibly important to check the combined gross vehicle weight rating (CGVWR) before hitting the road. Overloading the rig can cause equipment failure which may lead to an accident causing severe injury or death for all those aboard. Another downside is that backing up and securing the camper to the truck requires at least two people, unless the driver is very practiced and skilled.

Usually, this is a cumbersome process for the first few dozen of times one is learning how to properly secure the unit.

A subset of the truck camper class is a chassis-mounted camper. This alternative is where a camping unit is mounted directly onto the frame of a large truck. It is permanently affixed and cannot be removed like a conventional slide-in truck camper. Though this is a more expensive option, on the

positive side, often times this makes the whole experience more user friendly as the whole unit is much more stable when traveling off-road and while finding that perfect campsite off the beaten path! Typically, these units are slightly roomier inside than a mass-built truck camping unit and get about the same mileage. Often times, there is more storage as basement bays and larger holding tanks for water and waste are possible with this configuration.

On the downside, the unit cannot be easily removed and this makes the truck bed unusable. These rigs also tend to be more expensive than conventional truck camping units as they require some custom welding to affix the camper to the frame of the truck. Most aftermarket manufacturers charge upwards of $100,000 for these units. They have become extremely popular as a middle ground between those who travel on roads too rough for a truck camper but do not want the added expensive of a totally custom expedition rated RV (such as those built on a Mercedes Unimog or Zetros platforms). Often these RVs are capable of handling off road expeditions for weeks on end, and are very rugged, well built units.

On the downside, these camping units are almost as top-heavy as conventional slideout truck campers and can be difficult to drive when the wind blows hard. Again, always make sure the truck that will be carrying the camping unit has heavy-duty suspension and is capable of carrying the weight of the camper, plus gear, and people. During construction always determine the correct maximum load rating of the vehicle and be sure to stay well under this figure. The truck should have heavy-duty tires because having a blowout on a camping excursion is a horrible way to spend relaxation time!

Travel trailers are units designed to be towed by a car, truck, or van – depending on the overall size and weight of the RV. Travel trailers are much more comfortable than sleeping on the ground in a tent and the smallest units are not much larger. Travel trailers are the oldest type of RV dating back to the late 1800s when they were propelled by horses. Initially, these units were built for those who were constantly traveling and the wealthy, today they are among the most affordable of all RVs.

This category of RV provides all the modern comforts of any home such as a kitchen, bathing area, sleeping, dining and living facilities, electric and plumbing systems, and modern appliances in an increasingly more attractive, hard-walled package. Like all towable units, they can be unhitched from the tow vehicle which is then available to be utilized for convenient local travel to and from the campsite. One of the downsides to a travel trailer is that no passengers or pets are allowed inside during transit due to Department of Transportation regulations. This may be especially tricky if traveling with a large number of people for extended distances.

Travel trailers sleep as many as ten people with up to three slideouts. If the towing vehicle is already owned, a towable trailer remains one of the cheapest ways to start RVing. This is because just the living quarters need to be purchased, not a motor or drive-train. Because of this, travel trailers range from ten thousand on the low end to upwards of $80,000 for models that have all the bells and whistles. Towing is easier than ever before as units are becoming more and more lightweight with industry advances especially aluminum and composite building materials. Ultra light units may now be towed by the smallest cars without sacrificing the modern conveniences we have all come to appreciate.

Fifth-wheel trailers, as opposed to travel trailers, are solely designed to be towed by a pickup truck with a specially installed hitch in the bed of the vehicle. Fifth-wheels provide every day comforts such as a kitchen, multiple areas suitable for sleeping, dining and living facilities, electric and water systems, modern appliances and up to two full bathrooms. By their nature they all have bi-level (two floor) arrangements and the most luxurious feature up to five slideouts. Like all towable units, they can be unhitched from the tow vehicle which is then conveniently free for traveling to and

from the campsite. Fifth-wheels generally sleep at least six people in comfort and typically range from $15,000 to well over a hundred thousand dollars with the best amenities and options. These RVs are roomy featuring high ceilings and lots of storage space making these rigs very popular among full timing RVers and those traveling with the whole family.

One of the major benefits is that fifth-wheels tend to be more stable than similarly sized travel trailers as the pickup mounted hitch reduces trailer sway and reduces the combined length of the two vehicles while driving. These motorhomes are easier to maneuver when in reverse due to their unique tow connection. They also have more storage space then travel trailers, and can be easier and safer when towing than other types of travel trailers.

Fifth-wheels are considered to be among the best units for extended camping. Their size may even rival that of a two bedroom duplex apartment (due to the expansive living area and small set of stairs leading to the second floor) making them especially attractive to full-timers. Manufacturers have constructed vehicles that measure up to 15 feet wide (with the slideouts extended in particular sections) by 50 feet long, and some even feature a loft sleeping area or porch that slides out from the main structure! New advancements in the industry include multiple bedrooms and up to two full

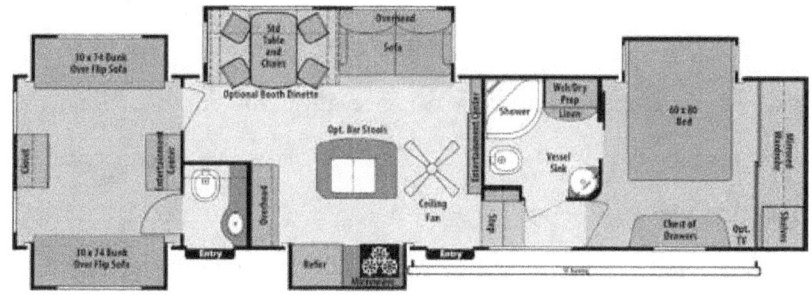

bathrooms. Most typically, the master bedroom is configured to be towards the front whereas the living areas are prominently featured in the mid-section or rear of the unit. The amenities may be as comprehensive and luxurious as the owner and their pocketbook are willing to bear. However, on the downside, the larger models can be among the most difficult RVs to maneuver. As such, they are not great for taking too far off major roadways and may be a hassle for novices.

Fifth-wheels are towed by full size trucks, with a fifth-wheel hitch mounted in the truck bed. This system is very close to what is used by full size commercial tractor trailer semi trucks. Fifth wheels are unique in that a portion of the unit extends over the rear of the pickup truck bed when being towed. This puts the hitch pivot point just ahead of the trucks rear axle, meaning that towing a fifth-wheel trailer is easier as the trailer tracks better due to the hitch point.

Toy haulers are another segment of the RV market and are available as motorized or non-motorized units. These RVs feature a built-in garage (most commonly towards the rear) for hauling motorized cycles, ATVs, sports equipment, or even small cars. Consider the extra weight of all the toys and the capacity of the tow vehicle when considering this option.

There are many manufacturers that specialize in these vehicles and they come in a very wide range of sizes and styles. Typically, the garage space is very versatile and most modern toy haulers feature a conversion kit that turns the garage into a guest bedroom, lounge space, or even an office when the RV is parked and the vehicles or toys removed. The most common models sleep between four and eight people and feature one or two slideouts. Prices range from $25,000 almost a quarter of a million in new condition.

While many people initially believe they want as large a RV as they are able to afford, length and width often determine the quality and number of spots to which the RV will be able to fit. If a specific campground or area is more appealing than others, find out any restrictions on RVs those places have and which they will be unable to accommodate. Make sure that when buying a larger RV, this will not be an issue. If a RV is chosen that is too long or too wide, it will not be able to safely navigate many country roads or those of smaller public campgrounds. This is especially true of those in the national forests and parks throughout much of North America such as the less tourist-oriented sections of Banff or Yellowstone.

Additionally, RVs with slideouts may not fit into many of the sites in these campgrounds with the rooms extended. Slideouts are great and dramatically increase the interior room within a RV. Most new RVs have several slideouts and they're extremely popular within the industry, but they do have a few specific drawbacks. Be careful of buying a model that prevents the RV from being used in the manner that it's intended. There are also other disadvantages to slideouts including their added weight which leads to decreased handling and worse fuel mileage. Be sure to make allowances when parking so the slideouts will not hit a tree or other campground equipment when extended. Extra precaution is needed to assure that severe damage to the motors or even the slideouts themselves is not sustained.

Slideout rooms are becoming more common as the technology for the motors and ancillary parts decrease in price. When parked, these motors slide out the room using an electric motors or hydraulic rams. This adds more space to the interior of the RV by opening up significantly more floor space. A slide out in the living room of an RV would commonly have the sofa and dinette within adding around 50 square feet to the living space. Some RVs have four or more slideouts and these features have even started to be offered in the bedrooms and bathrooms of many models.

Buying a RV is a major investment and it is important for buyers to make as well-educated and informed purchasing decision as possible. It's easy to overlook something and loose thousands of dollars or forget to check some features and even worse may end up with a RV that is not useable. Most importantly, buyers need to be knowledgeable about exactly what type of RV they are seeking and what features are most important for their lifestyle. Whatever the case may be, buyers should realize what they are looking for before buying. Because after purchasing, it will just be too late.

RVs come in numerous types, sizes and price ranges. Take the time to research specific needs and wants, factoring in how the vehicle will be utilized and how far everyone will be traveling, and the average length of time spent camping. Break the camping down into off-grid or boondocking time and time that the RV will be hooked up to electric, gas, water, sewer, and the like. The more time spent off-grid, the more the RV will have to be self-sufficient. This will limit the models that are available. For those who plan to travel cross-country, a motorized RV might make more sense than a towable. For those who plan to go camping off the beaten path, a small class B or truck camper will probably make more sense.

Regardless of which RV type and specific model is eventually decided upon, there have been numerous RV industry advancements in the past decade which have widespread application throughout the range of RVs. Nearly all categories have options which include slide-outs; solar and wind power; ultra-quiet and highly efficient generators; lightweight composites and fiberglass construction; a multitude of storage bays, satellite dishes that receive high definition television signals and broadband internet; ultra-low amperage modern appliances; programmable LED lighting and HVAC units that barely use any energy at all, and much more! All of these have had a significant impact on the industry and provide all the comforts of home in a package on wheels!

In the end, selecting the proper RV is a purely personal decision. It really doesn't matter whether a person selects a large bus conversion or a small popup trailer, as long as they are happy with the decision and it meets their particular needs and wants. Whether living in a RV in pure luxury or a model with just the basics, recent advancements have had a huge impact on the industry and have made purchasing the right RV easier. Regardless of the model chosen, buyers will feel more comfortable and more at home than ever before. Enjoy time spent living off the grid and spread the word to others. This lifestyle is available to almost anyone and is becoming more popular with every passing day as people realize the benefits outweigh the detractions.

SECURING A GREAT PURCHASE

Shopping for a RV is often fraught with apprehension and anxiety. Especially for those who are first time buyers. But, it need not be this way. There are great buys on recreational vehicles every day and for those who know enough general information about RVs, what they're looking for, and how to negotiate, they often score a great product at a phenomenal price!

The RV that is ultimately selected has to fit the needs, wants, and resources of its owner/s. All of these factors are highly personal and unique to an individual or family. These particulars are not easily quantified, but some general questions to help buyers shop are easily posed. Of course, this is just a short list because the list of potential questions is endless:

- ➢ What is the total budget?
- ➢ Is diesel or gas preferred?
- ➢ How many people will regularly be eating and sleeping in the RV?
- ➢ What is the right floor plan for the buyers needs?
- ➢ Which options are needed and which are wanted?
- ➢ Are one, two, three, or more beds necessary?
- ➢ Is the primary bed large enough to sleep comfortably?
- ➢ Will a split bathroom work better than a walk-through bathroom?
- ➢ Is there enough space in and around the bathroom for everyone?
- ➢ Is there enough counter space to comfortably prepare meals?
- ➢ Is there enough storage space to store all of the owners' belongings?
- ➢ Is a front, rear, or mid-coach kitchen desired?
- ➢ Is the entertaining space large enough to meet the owners' needs?
- ➢ Is the shower large enough?
- ➢ Are the holding tanks large enough for the type of camping desired?
- ➢ Are solar panels and large battery banks necessary or will a generator work?
- ➢ How many nights out of the year will be spent boondocking?
- ➢ Will pets come along and is there enough room for them?
- ➢ Will the RV spend more time on pavement or back country areas?
- ➢ Are there specific campground ordinances that need to be followed with this RV?

Once those questions are considered and answered, one of the next things to decide is whether to buy a new or used motorhome. This is a major consideration before purchasing and the two markets are very different. To assist with making this decision, think about how the RV will be utilized and consider any budgetary constraints. For those who are only planning to take a couple of weekend trips or use it for one week out of the year, a used RV might be best. This is due to several factors including upkeep and deprecation. But, remember it does not do anyone any good to own an RV if there isn't enough money left in the budget to enjoy it. Purchasing (including tax, title, and other fees) usually costs more than most people realize. And, after all those expenses are accounted for, do not forget that the RV needs to be supplied with bedroom linens, toiletries, cleaning supplies, as well as silverware and utensils for the kitchen along with much more. Having the comforts of home will make the journey much more enjoyable!

RV owners typically seek a layout that offers at least enough space so that six people can converse comfortably while seated, four are able to eat a meal with ease, and at last two are able to sleep comfortably throughout the night. Full time king and queen size beds are enough of an industry standard that owners should not have to compromise on available sleeping space or be required to slumber on a pull-out couch. However, if a small RV such as a class B or popup is decided upon, this may be a requirement. Typically, couches or convertible dinette sleeping arrangements are for the occasional guest, not for the owners. Over time, making the couch into a bed or converting the dining table every night will be prove to be a consummate annoyance.

Before deciding on and purchasing a suitable RV, narrow the choices down to a few suitable layouts and manufacturers. Make sure to choose a model that will work for everyone who will be spending time aboard. For instance, most senior citizens with grandkids end up traveling with at least a few extra passengers during the summer months and for those folks, it does not make sense to buy a model with just one bed. Pull out couches and convertible furniture will work just fine during these circumstances, as long as the coach has these options.

A good way to research what is available throughout the marketplace is to order brochures via mail, or just download them directly from the manufacturer webpages. Next, head to a RV show or dealership that features a wide range of manufacturers to confirm that the RV products are as great as the brochures make them seem. Make sure to buy from a manufacturer and, preferably, a dealership as well that will stand behind the product before and after the sale. Complete research into manufacturers on the Internet, request brochures of their line, take a factory tour or two, and attend local RV shows to learn more about all of the available options.

The vast majority of the RV expositions in North America are listed on the Recreational Vehicle Industry Association (RVIA) website. This group features a comprehensive calendar detailing shows in any particular area. RV shows are good for browsing and buying but also for learning about the RV lifestyle from those who know it well. When looking to buy a new RV this commentary can be especially useful. The RVIA website also lists approved dealers in any geographic location. Make sure to cross-reference area dealers with the Recreational Vehicle Dealers Association (RVDA) to determine the most reputable. Don't forget to read feedback from other consumers that have dealt with these dealerships. Individuals should pay particular attention those buyer reviews who have purchased a similar model compared with the one they are seeking.

While at the show, spend a large amount of time in each RV that is of interest. Follow up by stopping into a dealership and test driving the top three models to determine if they are of comfortable size. This is a purchase that will likely last many years, so not only does the RV need to be reasonably accommodating while driving down the road, everyone must be at ease spending many hours inside the RV. There will be rainy days when camping and waiting until inclement weather strikes is not the best time for deciding whether or not the interior space is sufficient.

While buyers are looking into a particular RV model, they should actually stand in the shower, sit down on all the chairs, lay down on the couches, open the drawers and cabinets, look into the wardrobe to determine whether there will be enough space for clothes. Check the height of the kitchen appliances and countertops, and look into the storage bays. Individuals should make sure not to buy a smaller motorhome than they will be comfortable in. If it's frustrating for someone to live in a smaller space than they're comfortable, they may give up the RVing lifestyle without giving it a real chance. If a particular RV is not comfortable for a short while, it will definitely not be comfortable for periods of extended camping. This rig needs to be comfortable to all parties that will be spending time in the RV, not just the decision maker or person who decides to purchase the coach. This is because if others are dissatisfied, it will eventually create friction and dissension and make everyone unhappy.

Really poke around the interior and exterior of the coach and decide if it's the right RV. If children will be spending time aboard, determine if they are comfortable with the particular layout and trim choices. These include the sleeping, dining, and lounge arrangements. Lots of kids for example, means that bunk beds may be needed as well as space for them to play. Such space may be found in a living room slideout, in a rear bedroom during the day, or even towards the middle of the coach. Some of the newer coach models even have small multipurpose rooms in their slideouts that may be used for a variety of purposes. Besides converting this space into an office, may folks use these areas as playrooms.

If small children or pets will be consistently aboard, it may sense to Scotch Guard furniture and carpeting, or otherwise treat them so they will be less susceptible to spills and other stains. Determine if there is enough space for those rainy days when the whole family will be inside playing cards or watching movies. Are there enough TVs so that the kids are able to watch their own programming and stay occupied without bothering the adults? If traveling with teenagers, make sure that the fridge and pantry are large enough. Are there separate bunking areas that may be closed off so older children feel as if they have enough personal space? If a family dinner is important, make sure there is enough room around the primary table so that everyone may eat at the same time and feel relaxed while doing so. Assure that the sleeping areas are comfortable for everyone, and that they have enough room to fully extend their arms and legs. Make sure that the lights are in acceptable places and are bright enough to cook, read, or write. Make sure the shower is of sufficient height and that headroom throughout the coach is ample for freedom of movement. Are end tables adjacent to the bed important? Make sure the RV has all the features for normal life that meet the needs of the purchaser.

A single person or couple will have priorities that will be vastly different from those traveling with a family. For those who love cooking, a kitchen with plenty on counter space, a residential style refrigerator, stove, and microwave may take priority. In addition, maybe a specialty wine fridge or hobby area will take precedence within the owners' living space.

While shopping for that perfect RV, pick up as many brochures and other product literature as possible. Many manufacturers will even send their literature directly to the potential buyer's mailbox or email them copies by request. Compare specifications, standard features, and optional equipment to determine what is most important. Bring along a notepad to make specific notes about the benefits and detractions of one model verses another. The features and trim that work well with one RV, may not mesh so well in another. Ask open-ended questions to pry as much information out of the sales personnel or product demonstrators as possible. A lot of pertinent information may be gleamed just from talking with others! After going through a host of different RVs, the details will likely begin to blend together, so notes will come in handy when thinking about the pros and cons of each model later on in the day or week.

After spending time at the RV show or dealership, go home and read through all the literature and any notes that were made during the visit. Study and compare the details unique to each manufacturer and model. Begin further narrowing down the features and specifications that are an absolute must, and merely those that will be nice to have. Often more options equal a greater cost. So, weigh optional specifications carefully to determine if they are necessary to the enjoyment of the RV lifestyle.

After selecting the final two or three choices, it's time to begin thinking about a timeframe for purchase, arranging the down payment, and securing any financing, if needed. The amount a buyer has to spend is determined by their total available cash. This figure is derived by the cash that the total amount of the monthly RV payment minus any monies that are contributed towards the down payment.

Negotiated RV purchase price

(−) Downpayment or trade-in

_____

= Loan amount

Loan amount

(÷) Number of months financed

_____

= Monthly payment

Buying the right RV is like buying a car and a house on the same day, only harder. It's more difficult in the sense that for most people this will be the second to third most costly purchase in their life after their primary residence. Some people, especially retirees even choose to purchase a RV that is more expensive than their fixed house in some cases! Regardless of the particular vehicle class, model, or price of the RV there are other considerations that are vitally important that are often overlooked. It is important to be aware of all the so called "hidden costs" in addition to the sticker price. These include ongoing maintenance, insurance, fuel and oil costs, parking and much more.

If any customization is needed, such as increased holding tank capacity, solar panels, extra batteries, or a wind generator, it's important to discuss this with the dealership at the time of purchase. Different dealers have vastly different costs for labor and the quotes for installation can vary by several hundred percent! Many times, they will offer to wire the solar panels or wind generator for free if purchased directly from their dealership. Or, they may offer additional battery capacity or an ancillary holding tank as an incentive to purchase. However, usually a dealership will have a higher markup percentage than other sellers. This financial cost, which is normally seen as a detraction, can be reconciled with better customer service and immediate access to the product. When ordering from a warehouse, consumers will likely have to wait several days for the product to arrive via mail carrier and the installation will typically be up to the consumer. The benefit of ordering from a warehouse is typically the prices are cheaper and there is a larger selection.

The primary difference between buying a RV and other vehicles is that motorhomes have less of a firm asking price. This means that the buyer need not be shy about asking for a very significant reduction at the time of purchase. The majority of RV dealers regularly add a considerable markup to the wholesale price. Do not fall prey to this aggressive strategy by determining a fair price before the negotiating begins. Buyers can expect a 20 to 30 percent discount off of the manufacturers suggested retail price (MSRP).

Most dealerships and individuals are willing to negotiate on the price, but not for the addition of custom designed and installed equipment. This is because these additions may take a significant financial investment on their part and a large amount of time to fix to the buyers' liking. Some folks selling real estate do not mind making such complicated concessions but it is unlikely in the RV marketplace. Be wary of this point before agreeing on a price. Buyers who are able to determine the actual wholesale price for new RVs and the current value of a used model will be much better off during negations. Use that number as a jumping off point, and try to stay as close to that ideal price as possible. Lastly, before signing always make sure that the prospective purchase is thoroughly reviewed by a certified RV technician or that the entire vehicle is covered under warranty.

A new RV generally is warranted from between from one to three years by the manufacturer with some dealerships offering additional warranties above and beyond that timeframe. Since they are more complicated it is no wonder that statistics indicate that new motorcoaches have more initial quality related issues needing to be fixed by the dealer than other types of vehicles. A RV is a very complex conveyance and is essentially the combination of a house and a vehicle rolled into one. This means that the probability of actually having a problem with one or more components is multiple times as common as just a house or automobile by themselves. The stove, sink, toilet, refrigerator are all appliances made by companies separate from the RV manufacturer who assembles all the parts together.

However, often the appliances and chassis carry their own warranties of up to several years. Typically, the manufacturer will deal with items under warranty and then talk with the original supplier directly to assure reimbursement. The RV manufacturer should stand by all of the items they assemble, even if they do not manufacture them in house. For instance, the engine and chassis frame are typically covered by the RV manufacturer for the first couple of years even though it may be built and delivered by Chevy, Ford, GMC, Freighliner, Mercedes, or whomever.

There are several different ways to purchase a motorhome. Buyers may visit RV shows, buy from dealerships, over the internet, or directly from private party sellers. Many people buy RVs from shows and this is one of the most popular and fun ways to purchase a new motorhome. However, this may not be the best bet as consumers are limited to the availability that is on site. Usually this means only one or two examples of a particular model will be on display. Buyers may not have the ability to buy a specific trim package and they may be limited as to the option packages that are available and able to be installed at the time of purchase. However, buyers may always visit a dealership or order parts directly from the manufacturer's warehouse for installation at a later date.

Buying from a RV show is an attractive and exciting option for many folks. This is why thousands of buyers every year commit to buying in this manner. But, make sure not to get caught up in the hype of the surrounding exuberance of the show's atmosphere and overspend or purchase a unit that is not ideal. Narrow the choices down to a few particular models. Once a particular motorhome is found to be appealing enough for purchase, take the time to arrange for preapproval of RV financing. When visiting a large RV show try to narrow the choices down at the beginning and decide upon one or two that meet specific budget goals and needs.

Representatives at RV shows are often very willing and excited sell their display RVs rather than have them driven back to their facilities. If prepared, well versed in the details, and relatively patient these floor models may be available at a substantial discount. When the show is coming to an end, buyers should check in on their favorite models again. If they are still sitting there unsold then it will be easier to be more aggressive with pricing. Buyers should explain their motivation and make several offers that day. Offer the dealer an aggressive price whatever that may be, and buyers who are in the ballpark should very quickly be a proud owner of a new RV at a discounted price.

As an alternative, the Internet may be a better solution and is becoming very popular with scores of individuals. Many people find that using the web offers more option availability and better pricing. Tens of thousands of motorhomes are available for purchase online at any given time and thousands are successfully sold via this medium every year. The downside is that more time is invested in finding the perfect RV. It's definitely easier and quicker to buy a RV at a substantial discount at a RV show, rather than doing the research online to find the perfect match. People are prone to take the easy way out, and this may hurt their finances in the long run. If securing the best price is important, than the Internet is likely the best place to shop.

Buying a RV online has become so streamlined it is now one of the greatest time savers to enter the marketplace in years. It has made the process of purchasing a RV much easier, quicker, and more straightforward. While individuals are sitting at home, or in their RV for that matter, they can easily navigate the information superhighway and digitally tour the majority of the available new and used RV inventory throughout North America or abroad. Dealers in Canada and the United States are proactive about constantly updating their inventory to make it easier for buyers to find the products they desire. Finding the right price and model has never been easier. Customers can more easily shop utilizing the resources available at no cost to them. Plus, future RV owners will find that sorting through the many choices is much less painful than in years past due to advanced searches and websites with vast databases.

Most sites list RVs for sale sorted by make, model, year of manufacture, price range, name of dealership, as well as those for sale by private party owners within a particular area. Once the RVs have been identified that meet the needs of their future owners, there are specific NADA guides geared towards the RV market. This will allow interested parties to enter the make, model, year and other pertinent details for a used RV and get an estimate of that vehicle's fair market value. While the NADA guides are commonly used by lenders and dealers to determine book value, keep in mind that buyers may acquire a deal considerably lower than the estimated value, particularly when buying directly from an eager seller. Comparison shop for those same makes and models of used RVs online (including the commonly overlooked RV sections of Craigslist and eBay) to determine how the book value compares to the pricing of similar vehicles throughout the marketplace. This will allow buyers to have a more accurate reflection of what percentage they can expect to negotiate off the sellers' asking price. It will also help determine fair market value. One of the downsides of purchasing online is that buyers need to be open to driving substantial distances to find the best deals. They will very rarely be found at the local RV dealership. Individuals need to be more selective about RVs that they consider buying because the time and gasoline costs can be significant when driving long distances to check out potential purchases.

There are two main ways to purchase an RV online. These include locating units that are regionally available to tour before purchasing and those that are not within driving distance, and need to be purchased sight unseen. To purchase the latter, typically the seller will conduct a virtual walkthrough over the Internet or phone. When buying online, prospective acquirers are able to narrow their search to suitable areas that are easily travel to in order to view, test, and negotiate the ultimate purchase price. This is by far the preferred method for buying a motorhome and makes it easier on both the buyer and seller. Face-to-face negotiation and final approval is still by far the preferred method for buyers. The Internet serves only to narrow search criteria and buyers use the dealer, RV show, or an individual seller's facilities and resources to actually purchase the motorhome. Most RVers will find that this is a simple, effective, and comfortable way of purchasing a RV.

Buying a motorhome sight unseen is a very controversial method. It involves the previous strategy but the trip to see the RV in person is skipped. This is not an ideal buying method but it can work well under the right circumstances. In many cases a deposit can be negotiated up front and returned if the actual RV doesn't match the description, pictures, and condition as it was presented. There are many people that have successfully purchased motorhomes completely sight unseen. But, buying a RV this way is not recommended for first time buyers because most do not know exactly what they're looking for. A few of the best websites to peruse while looking at the available new and used motorhome inventory are:

- RV Trader
- Camping World
- RV USA
- RVT
- Craigslist

- RV Online
- Camper Trader
- General RV
- Motorhome Directory
- Auto Trader

Regardless of the site one uses or if a listing ultimately leads to a purchase, definitely plant to utilize the Internet for research. It's a great resource and easy way to compare prices and make sure that the RV purchase is ultimately a good deal. There are many resources on the Internet for motorhome enthusiasts. A few of the most prominent RV review websites:

- Better RVing
- RV Advice
- RV Guide
- Trailer Life
- Motorhome

Unless the buyer is an expert in RVs they should try and buy from a reputable dealership. Factory approved RV dealers will have a professional staff that should look out for the consumer and offer fair pricing because they want repeat customers and positive reviews with the Better Business Bureau and other consumer advocacy groups. Trading fairly helps dealerships garnish strong, positive feedback to support continuing sales from the community. Don't be afraid to ask them to provide a tour of the grounds and service department. Check to see if they have certified technicians on site and determine whether they have any limitations to providing quality ongoing care for the particular recreational vehicle the buyer is interested in purchasing. Determine if they have the capability and facilities to do routine maintenance and warranty work on all of the units they sell. Look at their parts and accessories department. Do they offer a strong selection? Do they have a wide variety of RVs on the lot or are they quick to sell their inventory? How long have they been offering certain manufacturer brands and what is their general level of knowledge on those in which they specialize? How long have they been in business? A reputable dealership will make long term RV ownership much more pleasurable and share the best about RVing with their customers.

When buying from a dealer the number one rule is that all prices are negotiable. Many sales people are fantastically helpful, knowledgeable human beings. But one sour attitude or set of actions can spoil the reputation of an entire dealership. If buyers come across that bad egg they shouldn't be shy about asking for another sales person or locating a different dealer with better customer service. After all, they are there to serve the consumer and ultimately, if the buyer isn't happy, than that dealership will not be successful.

Many of the folks securing the best deals tend to buy at the end of RV season. Dealers typically pay fees every month a RV sits on their property. If buying at the right time these dealers will be more motivated than usual to move RVs off their lot. This is because they worry about having to wait out the winter while still making payments towards the principal. The more RVs that sit on the lot, the less space they will have for additional inventory. Inventory turnover is one of the most important tenants of sales. These factors combine to allow many of the best deals to be found during the early fall through the late winter months. This is when the remainder of the current year's inventory is being liquidated to make room for the newer motorhome models that are just being delivered by manufacturers.

One of the benefits of purchasing from a dealer is that many folks enjoy the convenience of an on-site campground. This is commonplace so that buyers may camp for a couple of days and nights and ask questions about their new RV as they arise.

RV dealerships are in business to make a profit from their sales. They remain in business by making a certain positive margin on every sale. That margin is usually several percentage points over the total purchase price which equates to thousands of dollars more than the wholesale market value of the RV. However, there are two good reasons for dealing with a RV dealership verses from a private party. The first is that they have access to the newest models and the widest range of options directly from the manufacturer. This is arranged through the "preferred dealer" network allowing buyers the greatest range of choices. The second is financing. When individuals are not able to pay cash or arrange other capital to be used towards a RV, a dealership is either the best option or sometimes, their last option. Dealers generally have access to hundreds of finance plans from dozens of institutions and should be able to qualify buyers into several of them. Buyers should easily qualify for a loan even if their credit history has blemishes.

Note that some dealers are able to offer better prices to those who choose to finance with them because they are able to make a little bit of money on top of the sale by underwriting the loan. There are three primary methods that allow dealers to profit by placing loans with consumers. The first is through "points" which is a percentage of the loan that they collect upfront. The second is by earning money by collecting interest and other "servicing" fees as the loan is processed throughout its lifetime. The third is by profiting when selling the loan to a servicing company, usually for an upfront fee or percentage of the total amount remaining on the note. Typically this fee is a percentage of the total profit the loan will bring throughout its lifetime. Keep this in mind during the throws of negotiation. After financing, one may always quickly pay off the loan to avoid finance charges.

The second reason for buying from a dealership is that most states have consumer protection laws in place that legally bind the dealership to allow buyers as many as three days to change their mind and cancel any deal. Of course, buyers should check and understand the applicable laws for the state in which they will be purchasing the motorhome. These laws allow buyers a small safety net in case of buyer's remorse or suddenly realizing that they cannot afford, don't need, or even cannot safely handle, say a motorhome that extremely long and wide.

Finally, RV dealerships are generally very thorough and give potential buyers all the information they can to orient them on the procedures for starting up, operating, and shutting down all the systems onboard the motorhome. This service is practically invaluable if the buyers are first-time RV owners and are accustomed only to fixed dwellings. There are many major differences between RVs and conventional homes that may confuse those who have never had an interaction with them before the buying process. Purchasers will rarely get that level of customer service from a private party and when they do there is no indication that it will be accurate. At least dealerships receive information, and sometimes training, directly from the manufacturer so their word is generally more reliable than the information which may be garnished from the public.

If there are several reputable dealerships in a buyer's area, one great tactic is to comparison shop by calling those dealers and asking for rock bottom price on a particular RV. Find out how long the price is good for and write down details of the call. The best deals are found during the colder months when dealers are clearing out the last of that year's inventory and receiving the newer model year RVs in stock. Every RV is a compromise in one way or another, but it's important to arrive at the right balance between the right features and an acceptable price.

The last method of purchasing a motorhome is to buy directly from a private party. Some people think it is worth their time to cruise through area RV parks and even residential neighborhoods to see if anyone is selling a rig in their driveway or yard. Depending on the area, some people will cruise around and see several used RVs with "for sale" signs on their dashboards. Though a significantly fewer number of people find their RV in this manner, sometimes the best deals may be found using this time intensive method.

Regardless of how the private party RV sale is found, buyers are much more likely to secure an amazing deal on a used RV if they are purchasing directly from the owner. Never assume, however, that the owner knows the true market value of their motorhome. The seller could be asking far too much or way under book value. Do all of the research beforehand and know the true market high and low average book values. Check out as many private party ads before negotiating to see what the asking prices are on similar RVs. When a RV is finally found that an individual may be interested in purchasing, set a firm appointment time with the owner.

However, do not just expect that everything will be hooked up and operating upon arrival. Kindly ask that it be done when setting the appointment with the current owner and that they demonstrate all features face-to-face. If the seller isn't willing to do that, look elsewhere for someone who is more amenable and easier to deal with. The folks who have the most problems are often the same that do not verify that every system is in working order before purchase. Remember that private party sales are always "as is" and the buyer has no expectation that current owners will be completely truthful or forthcoming about any problems. As the late American President, Ronald Reagan said, "trust but verify". It is great advice when making large purchases and certainly applies for this situation.

Often when buying from a private party, the owner will have maintenance records and even some dealerships will transfer paperwork from seller to buyer. This is especially true of upper end recreational vehicles and the ones that have been most lovingly cared for. Even better than securing these records from a private party seller is to have them transferred with the purchase directly from a dealer with a warranty that the RV is in sound condition. This limited warranty should cover at least the first few months of ownership, and preferably longer. Problem areas are usually improper roof maintenance, which results in leaks. Water intrusion from rain and snow can cause extensive and is sometimes hard to see. The resulting rotting and softening of structural parts may be found throughout the RV, not just along the roofline.

To combat leaking problems before they start, aim to stay away from RVs that have a flat roof. Always opt for a newer vehicle with a curved roof as that will help drainage, keep leaks at bay, and better structurally support tree limbs or snow that falls. Extra weight adds stress to a roof and those that are not curved or convex in shape will end up sagging over time. Just about every flat roof has problems, which is why modern manufacturing techniques have shied away from the practice of building them at all.

Previously owned RVs may be purchased for a fraction of the original price when sold by private parties. But, just because a used RV is cheap and has a low odometer reading does not necessarily equate to a good deal. This is because it may have just been sitting in the driveway or yard of the seller for years and have a host of issues. RVs like other vehicles require maintenance and when not done at proper intervals, start to degrade. The ones with a modicum of miles on the odometer may be more road-worthy and an overall better purchase.

Purchasing a unit directly from an individual may allow for an excellent price, but there are additional pitfalls to avoid. Don't buy a RV from a stranger without carefully researching the finance history and past ownership of that particular RV. Be sure to check the title, check it for any liens, and also have it looked over by a local RV technician. Remember that state sales tax must still be paid. In most cases this will require payment upon registration.

Dealers and RV show representatives have both fixed and variable costs that individuals do not have to bear. Many buyers find that purchasing directly from an individual offers a discount. However, even with the substantial savings there is seldom a guarantee or warranty of any kind. The majority of purchases will be "as-is". So, it is important for the buyers to know exactly the vehicle they're getting in exchange for their hard earned money.

These great finds are more commonplace because many individual sellers are simply looking to sell for enough money to pay off their existing motorhome loan. Buyers should keep an eye out for these deals as long as the original purchase price from the seller is reasonable. When buying a used motorhome, always get a seasoned RVer to look it over to determine if there are any problems.

This is especially the case when buying from a private party. Many problems may be avoided by following this simple key tenant.

Any major problems usually end up being deal killers. Sometimes conversations between buyers and sellers overlook the problems and the amount of money these issues will cost to fix. Whatever buyers think it's going to cost to fix a problem, it is likely less than half of the cost. If the work has to be done by a dealership or repair shop, it may cost much more! Any flaws that are found should be a solid bargaining chip for negotiating a lower offer price.

At the time of purchase, at a minimum be sure to ask for maintenance records, why the RV is being sold, find out if the RV has been properly winterized, and check the water delivery system for bacteria. Often this may be easily ascertained if the coach or holding tanks have a bad smell, but this is not necessarily the reason for bad smells, nor is bacteria always this easy to pinpoint.

Always test the actual coach on the road before purchasing. It's amazing how many people skip this crucial step before committing to purchase a particular unit. If a motorized RV is being purchased, be sure to drive it before buying. Driving a motorhome for the first time can be a little intimidating, but it's important that all drivers test its road worthiness before signing paperwork. Some owners want a motorhome that they feel particularly comfortable driving because they may be spending a lot of time behind the wheel. Check out all of the controls, the cockpit view, mirrors, and make sure the particular RV performs the way it was designed and how the owners need it to.

One of the final questions to decide before buying a motorhome is new verses used. This is a highly debated question and one that is ultimately up to the individual buyer. This controversy will live on long after an individual decision has been reached. Buyers may find discounts and great deals on used as well as new RVs. Sometimes, it's best to look for a brand new RV that is a model year older than the newest deliveries and make a deal on one of those units. Other folks feel they have received the best deal when buying a RV with very little mileage that has only been owned for a few months. Sometimes, these motorhomes have taken a huge depreciation hit and are still in their "like new" condition. It all comes down to personal buying preferences.

The advantage of buying a used RV is most often found in the reduced price. As the newer, more technologically advanced RVs come on the market, the older models become progressively cheaper as the months pass. Motorhomes are similar to all vehicles in that they start depreciating as soon as they are driven off the dealer lot. Many people find that used RVs are a far better value but they also could bring higher maintenance costs and could be more difficult to find replacement parts. In addition, banks find them less financially lucrative to underwrite and thus harder for the buyer to secure funding. There is a very large used RV market as many RVers trade in their coach for a newer model every few years. Unfortunately regardless of price, with a used RV buyers will never know its exact entire history. They don't always know where the coach has traveled and how it has been taken care of during that time. Damage and general wear and tear may be caused by traversing bumpy terrain, rock or dirt covered roads, water damage, or infrequent and improper maintenance. The prior owner could be trading in this RV for another due to any array of undesirable reasons.

Used motorcoaches have already taken a depreciation hit. This loss in value can be as much as 30% within the first year. Typically, the value decreases by over 50% in three years! Consequently, buying used can be a bargain bonanza for savvy shoppers. But, on the downside, some of these RVs have been abused and not maintained as well as they should have by the seller.

Buying a used RV that's still in good condition can save buyers real money. According to the website RVers Online, after factoring in depreciation, financing, maintenance and other costs, an RV that's three years old can cost half the price of a new model.

One method of determining the fair market value for a new recreational vehicle is to find the cost of a similar used model and add back the depreciation. For those that do not have the particular RV depreciation schedule, simply add back 25% for every two years the model is in age to determine the right figure. For example, let's say a one-year-old model is found in excellent condition. If a used model's fair market value is $48,000, to estimate the new FMV, multiply the used FMV by the depreciation percentage, as such: $48,000 * 1.25 = $64,000.

When negotiating the price of a new RV without having to determine the FMV in advance, at least remember that the MSRP's contain roughly a 30% markup for the dealer (actual markup can vary widely between brands and models). Let's say that an approximate 15% markup is determined as fair by both parties. In that case, take the MSRP and multiply it by the inverse of the markup, or 85%, to arrive at a target price. For example, if the MSRP is $105,000, the FMV formula will be: $105,000 * 0.85 = $89,250.

Before inspecting and test-driving a used RV, ask the owner or dealer about the condition of the vehicle, its history, title, warranties, repair and maintenance records. Another question of some importance is the reason why it is being sold. Try to pinpoint any potential issues during these conversations which may save on repair costs down the road. If there are problems that the seller knows about and is willing to disclose, the buyer may be able to have these fixed before the sale.

For a small fee buyers or sellers can purchase a vehicle history report. To do so, potential buyers will need the RVs 17-digit Vehicle Identification Number (VIN) to order the report. Depending on the vehicle's history and the data available, the report may include information on whether the vehicle has ever been damaged, rebuilt or stolen, as well as the manufacturer's specifications and any recall notices.

When test-driving a vehicle, ask the seller to have all mechanical systems fully operational and charged before arrival. Ask to test-drive the vehicle with the seller onboard to answer any questions as they arise. Let the seller do part of the driving as well. This will help the buyer see how the RV rides as a passenger and any subtle issues may be pinpointed at this time. Listen for noises and look for other problems that may not be as easily apparent while behind the wheel. It is certainly important to make sure the radio, CD / DVD / Bluray media players and all speakers are in working order. But, make sure not to complete the whole test drive with noise. That may hamper the ability to pinpoint problems. Test-drive the vehicle on different roadways, particularly at highway speeds on an open roadway, and find an empty parking lot to see how it backs up and handles in tight situations. Determine if the steering is pulling one way or another. If this is occurring, it may be a sign that the RV needs a wheel alignment or has suspension issues.

An RV with low mileage may or may not be a benefit for the buyer. This is because a used RVs with too few miles can be an indicator of a problem-prone vehicle or one that's difficult to drive. Additionally, motorhomes that have been parked and unused will almost always require extensive and expensive service. Some of the issues may include replacing belts, pumps, batteries, and tires. Other common issues that are much more expensive include rebuilding the generator carburetor or redoing the brake system. Another costly problem: leaks in the roof and other seams. If possible, some buyers choice to inspect and drive an RV during a downpour, preferably one with strong winds. This will not only help reveal leaks but give a better account of how the vehicle handles during harsh conditions. And, for those looking at used units that have spent some winters in cold climates and perhaps have not been properly winterized, be sure to check the plumbing for possible burst pipes, signs of rust, and other leakage.

Armed with information on fair market values, recent sales, prices for comparable vehicles, and a list of any problems with a specific vehicle, will support the case for offering a lower price than the asking figure. Offering to buy immediately and paying in cash can be a powerful bargaining chip. If financing is needed, it is usually more difficult to find a willing lender if the RV is beyond five years old. In some cases the lender will want to inspect and approve the used vehicle before offering to finance the loan.

Negotiating a great price on a recreational vehicle can be especially difficult during certain circumstances. This is because the profit percentage is typically higher for the dealer than on automobiles. Far more automobiles are sold every day than RVs and that industry is more competitive leading to lower prices. This means that dealers need to make a greater percentage on each RV to stay in business.

Anything that is found to be wrong with the RV may be used to benefit the buyer during the negotiations. Things that will need to be looked at more closely, or even have to be repaired should be pointed out to the sellers before agreeing to purchase. For example, if the tires are more than five years old, they will almost always need to be replaced regardless of their tread condition. Some of the potential problems are dry rot, separation of the rubber sections from one another, prior punctures that have been patched or otherwise repaired, and even tired that have been improperly inflated leading to an imbalance of rubber towards one side. Remember that there are tire codes with Department of Transportation specified numbers stamped on the sidewalls which correspond to a manufacturing date. Tires made after the year 2000 have a corresponding four-digit DOT code. The first two numbers represent the week in which the tire was manufactured. The second two represent the year. A tire with a DOT code of 1213 was made in the 12th week of 2013. It's vitally important to determine the age and condition of the tires because a new set of six (which is common) can run from $200 to $700 each! Buyers should figure they will spend at least $1,500 to replace their coach tires. The RV may not be such a great find if it immediately needs a new set of tires!

Other negotiating points include dirty carpets, appliances that have issues, stains on the upholstery or window treatments and much more. Excessive mileage on motorized RVs can also be a significant negotiation point - even on diesel products. Diesels can, and often do, have more mileage, but keep in mind if properly maintained can outlast gasoline engines by a large margin!

There is always wiggle room when buying a new RV and great deals can be had. This is especially true during the fall and winter months! Just like any other dealer, RV dealers have loans on inventory and are making monthly payments to a bank or other financial institution for all of the rigs on their lot. Every month that that RV sits on a dealer lot costs the dealership owner money in interest and advertising costs. All dealers want their products to sell and the quicker the better!

One of the best tactics for securing great deals is to play one dealer offer off of another. Secure a written quote from one potential dealer and shop that deal with their competitor dealers. Tell the other dealerships they need to beat the low price. If they cannot, buyers should almost always take the best deal. Buyers should always make sure they are comparing apples to apples meaning they need to make sure the RV is the same brand, model, specifications, and warranty. Specifics are key to getting the salesperson or the team to come down on their price point/s. If nothing else, have the dealer throw in some of the accessories or an extended warranty plan. Often dealerships will include a hitch, extra long sewer hoses, more efficient batteries, solar panels, and more to seal the deal with the buyer.

Make sure to check out the dealers BBB rating, making note of any unresolved complaints, and check the repair department before signing. If possible, talk with other customers about their experiences with the same dealer. The buyers' relationship with the dealer rarely ends the first time they drive off the lot. This is because repairs and maintenance are very important to the overall RV experience. Assure the dealer representatives are efficient, friendly, organized, and outgoing because nobody likes being hassled when it comes time to get repairs or warranty work completed in a timely manner!

Acquiring a factory fresh recreational vehicle typically means the owner will have less maintenance issues initially and they will also receive some type of warranty from the manufacturer. The downside to purchasing new is that RVs tend to depreciate at a more rapid pace than other vehicle types. There is something special about driving off the lot with a brand new RV that has never been owned by anyone else. It's a special feeling, but not necessarily worth the additional cost. However, having the previous owner take the depreciation hit on a used motorhome may just be worth settling for a model that is slightly older or has a few more miles on the engine.

If any doubts surface as to whether motorhoming is the right step, rent before buying. Many folks are so excited for a change that they purchase a RV impulsively. The purchaser should take time in selecting the ideal coach and assure that it has most of things they need to have in a motorhome. Purchase a buyer's guide or visit the manufacturer's website that offer feature lists and floor plans. Be patient while purchasing and make sure it's the ideal RV for buying. Waiting may be required to secure the best models. Choose the best manufacturer and layout first and then all bells and whistles afterward. Optional features have proven to be much less important towards owner satisfaction ratings and are thus, usually less crucial.

After the sale, it's important to reregister the vehicle, take care of insurance, and pay any sales, title, transfer, and other applicable taxes. If buying new, the dealership or RV show representatives should be responsible for registering the vehicle. If buying from a private owner, typically the buyer will be responsible for registration. When it comes to insurance make sure to receive confirmation of coverage before taking delivery. Many times, insurance companies will even email or make proof of insurance available for printing directly from their website. Some companies have even begun to offer smartphone applications that detail insurance coverage.

There are several great tax advantages to purchasing a RV. First, the interest is deductible as a motorhome qualifies for the mortgage deduction. In the eyes of the IRS, it is legally a "second home". Discuss any pertinent details with a tax adviser or legal counsel but, just about everyone will qualify for this significant deduction.

The second primary advantage is that virtually any state will allow RV owners to qualify as official residents. Being able to call any state "home" for tax purposes may result in a significant savings at tax time. There are many benefits to being a resident of one particular state instead of another. A certified tax adviser will be able to expand upon the details. The most popular states for fulltime RVers to select as a domicile are South Dakota, Texas, and Florida. There are many reasons for these choices. Chief among them is that none of these states have a personal income tax. In addition, vehicle registration fees are reasonable, and importantly, they allow the use of a mail forwarding address as a legal address for such things as driver's licenses, vehicle registration, and other legal documentation. Not all states allow this privilege for their residents and it's of great benefit to RVers who are constantly traveling. These states also have a low barrier towards permanent residence and it's not paperwork intensive to do so. None of those three require any physical time in the state, while many other states do. Other RVers have different criteria. For instance, Alaska residents receive a share of the state's Permanent Oil Fund Dividend, which is typically well over one thousand dollars per annum, per resident.

Make a list of the priorities that are needed in a motorhome and search for the right one within that price range. Remember, that the first coach purchased probably will not be the buyers' dream coach, nor will it be the only recreational vehicle they ever purchase. Make sure to do enough research before buying a motorhome. Surf the Internet, attend rallies, take seminars, and talk with motorhome owners before making a final decision on which motorhome to buy. Folks should purchase a coach just they would buy a house with growing children. Ideally, it should be a little larger than is needed today, but not too large as to be overwhelming at any point down the road.

If full-timing in the new RV make sure not to sell the primary residence until after having traveled for a couple of years. At the minimum, buy a used motorhome and use it for a season or two. Individuals will then have a better idea of what to look for in their ideal motorhome without having to sell all of their belongings or renting a storage unit.

Before starting off along the journey, be patient, plan for ample fun, drive safely, and actually read and understand the owner's manual and other literature that came with the RV. Individuals should learn all they can about the motor, transmission, rear end, brakes, exhaust system, air intake, carburetor, and intake manifold — the things that actually make the vehicle work. This way, when something goes awry they will have a better understanding of what to expect, how the problem will be fixed and how much it will cost.

It might happen that when an individual finds a really nice RV where everything works, the price is right, and it seems like a good value. But, for whatever reason, that person did not choose to make an offer quickly enough to close the deal before someone else snapped up the motorhome. Consequently, it gets sold to another interested party. This will surely be disappointing, but buyers must let this one deal pass and move on as if it never happened. Otherwise, they are at risk of jumping on the very next deal that comes along, no matter how negative the terms or how poorly the next model fits their lifestyle. This is because individuals who feel like they have just lost out on a great buy tend to reason that they may lose out to yet another great buy and overbid or hastily buy this other RV. In these situations, emotions take over and good judgment flies right out the window. Those who make a hasty decision to buy, are almost certain to regret it. They should expect to come down with a serious case of buyer's remorse after buying this RV that was not a great deal. Do the requisite research and do not be taken as an overly aggressive buyer.

The bottom line is to be patient. Use more thought than emotion and shop a combination of private party sales and RV dealerships to find the best deal. That's the best game plan for securing the very best deal on a new or used RV and saying "goodbye" to buyer's remorse.

Those living in colder climates should try shopping for their new RV in the fall and winter months when the camping season is over. Many RV owners and dealers are looking to offload their rigs at cheaper prices, since there isn't much demand for camping in the winter months in certain areas and many current owners do not want to deal with the maintenance and storage.

Existing RV owners are usually older and wiser. Look for an RV park close by, go there, and walk around. Feel free to pose questions to current owners when someone friendly comes around. Most RVers love to share their knowledge with others and this is a great way to find out more information about a potential purchase before buying! Of course, everyone will have different opinions about different products, but a general consensus should begin to emerge and this will help with the final purchase decision.

The more research a potential buyer does before the purchase the happier they will be after the sale is completed. There are many good internet sites to determine value, issues, and expectations about almost any RV in which a person may be interested. Most sites include many links to specific areas of interest and answers to many of the questions buyers have about their RVs.

Everyone who owns a RV should intend to use it as much as possible. Otherwise it's just an oversize unnecessary purchase and will just take up valuable driveway or lawn space. So pack up the coach, the kids and the pets, and head out to explore the wonderful lands all around the region and beyond! RVs are a wonderful way to see the continent and there are so many great places to visit and explore. Take the time to build some lasting memories with family and friends and enjoy the journey to its fullest!

DIESEL VERSES GASOLINE

Whether driving for just an hour to reach a local campground or across country for that ideal spot, it's very important to determine whether a gasoline or diesel engine will be more suitable. The choice will affect which manufacturers are more desirable and which models best fit the individual needs and personal preferences of the buyer. Though gasoline is much more common in North America, drivers in much of Asia and Europe frequently choose diesel over gasoline for its rich torque output and higher fuel efficiency. Diesel engines can typically pull more weight efficiently than their gasoline counterparts of the same size. This will allow for longer, heavier RVs with more optional features and a greater towing capacity.

The most significant cost for RVers is their fuel costs and their rigs do not get good gas mileage. Usually motorcoaches realize between five a ten miles per gallon for gasoline engines and ten to 14 mpg for diesel. Towables decrease the efficiency of the vehicle by at least five to 15 miles per gallon. Some of the largest and heaviest fifth wheels get even worse mileage. Smaller class B vehicles will obviously secure much better mileage than their larger class A and bus conversion counterparts. Diesel engines have a larger upfront cost, but they are far more efficient in the longer run. For daily drivers, this savings can equate to a difference of several hundred dollars per month in fuel costs - at a minimum!

In theory, a diesel engine is very similar to that of gasoline. They both run off the process of internal combustion and both are designed to convert the compressed chemical energy within the fuel into mechanical energy. This mechanical energy forces rods to moves pistons up and down inside cylinders. The pistons are connected to a crankshaft, and the up-and-down motion of the pistons, known as linear motion, creates the rotary motion needed to turn the wheels of a vehicle and propel it in any direction the driver chooses.

Diesel and gasoline engines both covert fuels into useable energy through a series of small explosions inside the engine known as combustions. The major difference between diesel and gasoline is the way these explosions occur. In a gasoline engine, fuel is mixed with air which is then compressed by pistons and ignited by sparks. These sparks are derived from a series of small devices known as spark plugs. Conversely, in a diesel engine, the air is compressed first, and then the fuel is injected into the cylinders. Because air heats up when it's compressed, the fuel ignites and propels the process.

Another major difference between diesel and gasoline engines is found during the injection process. Most car engines use a port injection or carburetor. A port injection structure injects fuel just prior to the intake stroke. This is done outside the cylinder. Subsequently, a carburetor mixes air and fuel long before the air enters the cylinder. In a typical gasoline engine all of the fuel is injected into the cylinders during the intake stroke process and subsequently compressed. This density of the air and fuel mixture limits the compression ratio of the engine. If the procedure compresses the air too much, the air and fuel mixture spontaneously ignites and causes knocking. Because this process causes excessive heat, knocking can damage the engine. This is why knocking sounds are synonymous with engine trouble.

Diesel engines use direct fuel injection where the diesel fuel is injected directly into the cylinders. The injector on a diesel engine is its most complex component and has been the subject of a great deal of scientific experimentation. In any particular engine, the injector may be located in a variety of places. This component has to be able to withstand the temperature and pressure inside the cylinder and still deliver the fuel in a vapor suitable for combustion. Getting the vapor to a point where it is circulated in the cylinder so that it is evenly distributed is also an issue. To combat this problem, some diesel engines employ specialized induction valves and pre-combustion chambers to spin the air in the combustion chamber. This also helps to improve the ignition and combustion process.

There is also a huge difference between the two differing fuel types. All petroleum fuels start off as crude oil that's naturally found within the Earth. When crude oil is processed, throughout the refining process, it is most often separated into several different kinds of fuels. The most common include gasoline, jet fuel, kerosene and, of course, diesel. When comparing diesel fuel and gasoline, it's easy to tell that they are quite different. They certainly smell different and diesel is heavier and oilier. It evaporates much more slowly than gasoline and actually has a higher boiling point than water. Diesel fuel evaporates more slowly because its comparable volume is heavier. Specifically, its chemical combination is quite different in that it contains more carbon atoms in significantly longer chains than gasoline. Scientifically, gasoline is typically written in the chemical formula of C_9H_{20}, whereas diesel fuel is typically $C_{14}H_{30}$. It takes less refining to create diesel fuel, which is why it is historically much cheaper than gasoline. Since 2004, however, demand for diesel has risen for several reasons, including increased industrialization and construction in China and the United States. Due to the large amount of vehicles that now require diesel it is typically more expensive than gasoline.

Diesel fuel is used to provide power for a wide variety of vehicles and operations. Of course diesel fuels most of the trucks that individuals see driving along the highway. But it also helps propel boats, school and transport buses, trains, cranes, farming equipment, and heavy emergency response vehicles such as ambulances and fire trucks. It's also very popular for use in powering generators. Diesel is integral to the world economy. Without its high efficiency, both the construction industry and farming businesses would suffer immense financial losses with lower power and efficiency output. To boot, well over 90 percent of freight, whether it is shipped via trucks, trains, or boats, relies on diesel fuels.

Diesel fuel is arguably better for the environment when compared to gasoline. One of the benefits of diesel is that it produces fewer greenhouse gases than gasoline propulsion. Modern automakers have developed an increasing number of solutions that bring together an array of advanced technologies to create the world's cleanest fuel-burning automobiles. Advanced and highly precise components, from high-pressure fuel injection to a variable-vane turbo, create a more complete and powerful engine combustion. Some manufactures are beginning to release diesel engines that turn exhaust into harmless nitrogen and oxygen, rather than nitrogen oxide. Modern diesel engines can use both ultralow-sulfur fuels, which are now standard in Canada and the United States, or even B5 Biodiesel without having to worry about engine damage or related performance issues!

Direct injection devices are frequently controlled by advanced computer systems. These monitor fuel combustion while increasing efficiency and reducing carbon emissions. As diesel technology advances, better refined fuels such as ultra low sulfur diesel (ULSD) will continue to lower the amount of harmful emissions that are released into the atmosphere. Additionally, upgrading engines to make them compatible with cleaner fuel is becoming a simpler process. Other technologies such as continuously regenerating trap (CRT) particulate filters and catalytic converters reduce the exhaust particulate matter and burn soot comprised of carbon monoxide and hydrocarbons. This process reduces the environmental footprint of these engines by at least 90 percent!

Diesels engines simply get better mileage when compared with their gasoline propelled counterparts. These engines deliver an improved fuel economy of up to 30 percent over gasoline engines with a stronger torque performance. Diesels can also deliver as much or more fuel economy and torque when compared to traditional gasoline-electric hybrids. This improvement depends on the particular model, engine calibration, and such in an industry which is rapidly developing ever more efficient automotive technologies. Even if prices rise, diesel fuel would have to be at least 30 percent more expensive than gas to erase the cost advantages that a diesel engine's greater fuel efficiency provides.

Diesel is one of the most energy dense and efficient fuels available in the marketplace. Because it contains more usable energy than gasoline, it delivers better fuel economy with the same volume. Another benefit of diesels is that the engine does not have spark plugs or distributors. Therefore, they never need ignition tune-ups like their gasoline and alternative fuel counterparts.

Furthermore, diesel engines are built more ruggedly to withstand the rigors of higher compression ratios. Consequently, they usually last much longer than engines powered by other fuels before they require major repairs. Mercedes-Benz holds the longevity record with several vehicles clocking more than one million miles on their original engines! Consumers may not want to hang onto the same vehicle for that drastically long length of time. However, longevity and dependability definitely help assure high trade-in and resale values as well as piece of mind on the road!

Because of its fuel burning method, a diesel engine provides far more torque to the driveshaft than does a gasoline engine. As a result, most modern diesel passenger cars are much faster from a standing start than their gas-powered counterparts. What's more, diesel-powered trucks, SUVs, and cars also can out-tow gas-powered vehicles while still delivering the improved fuel economy that is of utmost importance in the marketplace today.

The layout of a diesel RV may be very different from that of a gasoline coach. One of the benefits of having a diesel engine is that many manufacturers offer it in the back of the rig allowing for much quieter driving. There are many more so called diesel "pusher" models where this engine is located in the rear of the coach. This is as opposed to RVs that pull the chassis and frame with an engine located in the front, like a conventional automobile. One of the detractions of this layout is that sometimes it is more difficult to work on the engine that is located under the rear bedroom. This can make engine maintenance harder for the do-it-yourself weekend mechanic as well as more expensive for professional jobs that bill by the hour.

Diesel technology is constantly being improved. Some of the smallest class B RVs built on the Mercedes Sprinter chassis realize up to 22 miles per gallon through most still realize a significant improvement in fuel economy and fall between the ranges of 16 to 18 mpg. Governments, especially the European Union and the United States, have placed increased pressure on manufacturers to produce low-emission diesel engines for passenger vehicles, trucks, buses, farm machinery, and construction equipment. With an efficient diesel RV, it's exciting to be at the forefront of innovation, engineering, and environmental friendliness. These regulations have resulted not only in low-sulfur diesel fuels but also specialized catalytic converters, advanced filters, and other devices to deplete or destroy toxic emissions. As technologies progress, diesel fuel will only become more efficient and cleaner burning. It is no wonder that diesel burning engines have been selling better and better every year!

PRE-PURCHASE INSPECTION

It's easy to get caught up in the moment and start fantasizing about the good times while cruising down a scenic highway in ones new home-away-from-home. Because daydreams often have a way of encroaching on reality, make sure to do all the necessary research before buying. Talk with other RVers as most are eager to share their stories and advice. There are several popular websites and online forums where RV enthusiasts chat, swap advice, and offer tips for buying RVs. Some of these include RV.net which is sponsored by the Good Sam Club. This is the world's largest organization of recreational vehicle owners. Other excellent references sites are available as well such as RVforum and RVtravel. Many of the sites post nationwide directories of RV clubs, shows, and rallies. There are even clubs for owners of specific RV brands such as the Winnebago Itasca Travelers (WIT). This is one of the largest manufacturer specific clubs boasting over 14,000 members who are interested in RVing caravans, entertainment, seminars and much more. These groups are often a great place to find out more about specific makes and models buyers are most interested.

If possible, have a trustworthy RV mechanic go through a potential purchase, especially check the "systems" (heating, AC, electrical, plumbing, etc.). These can become bottomless money pits if they have been maintained improperly or not at all. RVs can even deteriorate to the point they no longer function as designed. To combat any issues before they begin, there are several pro-active steps buying can take. Do not fall prey to high-pressure salesmen who aim to convince buyers that the RVs on their lot are the absolute best on the market. Always maintain an awareness of better RVs that perhaps are being sold by other folks. There are so many great deals to be found online, in the newspaper, or within a local community. Sometimes, a nearly-new RV is being sold at a bargain price because of a sickness or death or often times, a couple has simply become too old or out of shape to enjoy their purchase.

Inspecting the RV, preferably without the sales guy around is extremely important prior to purchase. Look inside, underneath, and around the entire RV. Look for doors and cupboards that don't stay closed, wires or water pipes running through holes that aren't protected with rubber grommets might quickly wear out. Construction debris under the dinette or inside closets is sloppy workmanship! Give the RV an inspection with a critical eye towards current problems. Compare this coach with another similar model and compare the craftsmanship and quality. Buyers quickly spot real differences in the way some are made and the pride that some assemblies take in their work.

When checking out a particular RV that is for sale, ask the seller to demonstrate that all the features work and how they do so. Make sure the fridge, stove, awning, toilets, water pump, as well as other appliances and fixtures are properly working. Look inside closets, cabinets, etc. and check for roof leaks. Water leaks cause dry rot in the walls and framing of an RV and can be terribly expensive to repair. Leaks are usually pretty easy to spot. Water damage evidence usually lies within and is easily noticeable by discolored patches in the walls and/or ceiling, but this is not always the case.

Always pay special attention to the sidewalls of a RV when purchasing. Some manufacturers do not spend much time on their construction and use cheap materials that often degrade over time. This is especially true of RVs that have been subjected to rough environments. RV grade aluminum siding is a classic material used in construction. It's durable, long lasting and inexpensive while being easy to replace if damaged. Another common material is fiberglass siding. Usually this is comprised of plastic sheets that are finished in either a medium or high gloss gel coat finish. Coated fiberglass is an extremely durable finishing method and can last many years with proper care and maintenance. Decals are the least preferable exterior RV design because they are not durable and are particularly susceptible to weather conditions such as sunlight, strong winds, and excess heat and cold climates. RV decals can shrink and change colors over time and are a cheaper alternative to a well-applied paint job. Peeling along the edges is common after just a couple of years of normal use. Buyers should seek out manufacturers that offer multiple coats of paint or clear coat which is much more durable. This offers the absolute best depth of gloss and shine that is only achieved with multiple coats of paint. Always aim for a manufacturer with certified technicians that know how to properly apply these coatings.

The most well built RVs are comprised primarily of aluminum where all of the joints are intricately fit welded to each other. This process is much stronger and longer lasting than spot welding or using screws and bolts to affix one section to another. The best RVs are constructed of welded tubes with laser cut joints. This is the most intricate and durable method of affixing to pieces together and lasts the longest while being less susceptible to wear and tear while jarring the RV as it drives down the road. Laser welded metal tubing has stronger joints with the best fit when compared with less precisely cut pieces of metal. An outdated method of welding uses butt-joints which require much more welding for an overall weaker fit. Every year, the RV industry uses less and less of this type of welding. Even though this more precise laser cut metal tubing is more expensive, buyers should opt for this construction method. Buyers should beware of older RVs and shy away from those that use the cheaper and less precise method. Joints that are not fit together as snugly will lead to a more bumpy travel and more often belongings will get banged around or even fall out of drawers and cabinetry that are constructed with this method.

The framework for the walls in less well constructed RVs may be as simple as two or three studs that have been nailed or bolted together, with the interior walls and exterior walls screwed or fastened to the aluminum, fiberglass, or wood. Some RVs utilize a laminate construction comprised of foam sandwiched between glued sheets of fiberglass on one side (typically the exterior) and wood luan on the (interior) side. Luan is a type of cheap plywood that is used as a type of wood paneling. The aluminum frame can be part of the laminated wall panels, and when the laminated sheets are cured under pressure, they become solid, light weight, and strong building blocks for RVs. Insulation between the walls can be fiberglass batting, foam sheets or urethane foam on less well constructed RVs. The roofline is often comprised of wood studs with luan on top. Then a covering of seamless rubber-like material called TPO of EDPM is applied, which is long lasting, water proof and durable. These roofing materials needs to be checked for cracks, leaks, and any damage at least once a year and should be cleaned at least once a season and ideally more often. The roof sealant needs to be checked on a periodic basis (at least annually) and if cracked or missing sections, redone with either a Butyl Sealant or EternaBond tape.

Unfortunately, the number one issue with used RVs is their lack of care and routine maintenance. This is especially true of the roof and exterior sidewalls. Especially on older RVs, if these are not inspected fairly frequently during the life of the RV, the sealant that keeps the seams from leaking will dry out. This typically leads to water from rain and melting snow to penetrate the roof. This often leads to the dreaded "roof rot" and will warp, dry rot, and generally cause the failure of the roof. This process can also lead to damage to the other wood products on board such as wall board, flooring, and structural parts of the RV. Water damage is costly and very serious in terms of having to literally rebuild parts of the RV that have been damaged in this manner. Not just wood framed RVs are affected, as most RVs contain wood in the floors, walls, or along the roofline. Sometimes, this even includes RVs that have been built touting "all aluminum" construction. RVs with true one piece roofs, including aluminum sheets or fiberglass construction can still leak if not properly resealed whenever maintenance work is done or sufficient time passes.

When getting serious about buying a particular RV, get up on a ladder and check out all four sides of the roof, including the roofline above any slideout rooms. Take the time to inspect every foot of the roofline and be careful. It is likely that the roofline will be curved in sections for aerodynamic purposes and there are most likely several "vent" pipes for the plumbing. Drains from sinks, toilets, and other miscellaneous items all require venting for proper use. There will also commonly be a refrigerator roof vent which is a four to six inch high rectangular vent and the newer models commonly feature skylights which are not strong enough to support the weight of an adult. Make sure all of these areas are in good shape and properly sealed at the base. There should also be an air conditioner shroud which covers the unit and protects it from the elements. Most RVs have a TV antenna that cranks up and down from the living room, through some are permanently mounted. Alternatively, there may be a satellite dish, while some RVs have both. This way, they are able to pickup local channels over the air while still receiving their favorite shows nationwide via the satellite dish for specialty networks. Some RVs also have a radio antenna mounted to the roof for better reception. All these things (except the A/C) should be clearly sealed with a black or gray caulking sealant, or at a bare minimum, extra strength all-weather tape.

When walking through the interior pay close attention to the walls and ceilings as they are usually the first to show signs of a water leak. The signs of an RV that is leaking and/or has in the past leaked, include discolored or warped wallboard, mold or rust colored stains on the ceiling, and flooring areas. Feel along the roofline and along the main sections of the interior walls. If there is a "give" any areas when pressure is applied, or a crunching noise than there is a major interior water problem! The air conditioner on the roof has a four inch thick foam seal that fits under the A/C unit and seals water out of the RV. This seal needs to be replaced whenever tightening the bolts. This area is found down inside the RV on the ceiling under the A/C grill. If it is not installed in a proper fashion than it will no longer stop the rain from leaking into the RV. This is another seriously neglected water intrusion point that can cause major damage to the roof and walls of the vehicle! If buying used, RVs with these signs are best left behind. Even for those owners who adapt at maintenance or even a craftsman, it would be expensive and labor intensive repair work to complete oneself. Double check the vehicle history report for any water damage and turn down the deal if there is verifiable information of environmental damage.

Pay extra attention to the exterior of the RV for damage including missing items such as storage hatches, covers for the refrigerator vent/s, water heater/s or furnace covers and doors. Are there any signs of leaking sinks in either the kitchen or bath? Check to see if there are any dented aluminum panels or damaged fiberglass. This includes whether the structure is faded or missing. Excess pieces may indicate that the panels were repaired or replaced potentially indicating a larger problem. Look for any other missing panels, torn or faded paint, decals, and graphics. Rusty frames and folding steps are commonplace among RVs that are older than a decade, but may easily be replaced. Rustoleum takes care of this issue and is not an expensive or daunting task for the weekend home improvement hobbyist.

Some of the more hastily designed and built brands of trailers and fifth wheels feature wood frame construction and these in particular have a real problem with leaking. Determining where the water is actually coming into the RV is very difficult because where it comes in on the outside is usually very different from where it appears on the inside. This is due to the insulation, electrical wiring, HVAC systems, and other products between the walls. For this reason, typically fiberglass framed RVs are a better purchase and typically have less leakage problems. Tour the plants where the RVs are built and usually the RV manufacturer will provide a water test of one sort or another upon request. This testing shows customers the durability of the new products, but will also educate consumers and serve as a knowledge base when they are testing other RVs for potential purchase down the road.

While at the factory it also makes sense to pay attention to the construction of the interior including cabinetry. Examine the thickness and type of wood and see how it is finished and detailed throughout the installation process. Do the doors and cabinet drawers and doors remain closed even when on hills and when driving? There are many ways of constructing RV drawers. The best manufacturers choose to use metal, full-extension drawer glides. This is as opposed to plastic components that wear out and easily break over time. The latter are not as durable and can even lead to drawers breaking when driving over rough road conditions. It is a much larger pain to have everything fall out of a drawer while driving down the road, than it would be to have a drawer extension break in a fixed dwelling.

Make sure the cabinets are well constructed and that they lock and stay closed while driving. Check to see if any of the cabinets are warped or damaged from water leaks. Be especially aware of this issue because many of the older and more cheaply built RVs use particle board, which absorbs water and falls apart over time. The same is true with the flooring. Seek out any soft spots, sags, humps, squeaks, and groans as these will indicate past and potentially future issues.

Do all the lights and their applicable switches work properly? If not, determine if there is an electrical issue, a blown fuse, or even simply a light bulb that needs to be replaced. Wiring can come loose over time if it is not properly installed due to jarring road conditions. Sometimes mice and other small creatures can even eat though electrical components that are not properly insulated and in a secure section of the RV where it is the hardest to replace. It all comes down to the fact that manufacturers who take the time and put in the extra work will simply have a better finished product.

Slideouts should operate without any grinding or squeaking noises or laborious groaning sounds. Among the more complicated mechanical features of newer RVs include slideout rooms. Do the slideout rooms seal fully or is daylight visible around the slideout edges? If light can be seen coming through the seals this means significant air is flowing between the RV and the environment outside. This can lead to problems with uneven heating, cooling, and moisture concentrating around the specific areas where there is air leakage. These areas can let in naturally occurring humidity in the environment further damaging the RV. Check when the slide is open and closed as there could be problems with one or another, but not both. When sl8ides are not properly balanced or overweight, sometimes they will sag due to gravity, causing major issues in the future.

There are also space concessions within the ideal RV with which to contend. Does the sofa make into a bed? If so, try out these extra sleeping areas and make sure they are comfortable and without wear. Some convertible couches have airbeds that inflate and deflate with the flip of a switch. Does this sleeping area stay properly inflated? Cheaper components (such as air pumps) can be overwhelmed due to the extreme changes in altitude and air pressure to which some RV owners subject these devices. Do the sleeping surface have any holes or repairs that will impair the bed from properly inflated or staying full for an extended period of time? Due to constantly changing atmospheric conditions, blowouts are common in air beds within RVs.

Test all kitchen appliances including the stove and oven (if the RV is so equipped), microwave, stovetop vent fan, and refrigerator. Assure that the refrigerator gets properly cold and that the freezer is working and running properly on both gas and electricity. The sink should have hot and cold running water. The holding tanks including those for the water heater, fresh water, gray water, and black water should be free from corrosion and there should not be indicator lights warning of problems. Check other monitoring systems to assure they are working properly as well. Test the holding tanks by filling and emptying all of them at least once. This includes the black, gray, and white water tanks.

The bathroom sink needs to have both hot and cold running water, properly flushing toilet, and a shower that quickly turns from cold to hot at the turn of a switch. Assure that the ceiling vent opens and closes with the fan working (without making improper noises) and that there are no signs of leaks around the fan or vent.

Most hoses and holding tanks are located in the basement of a RV. Those folks who will be traveling in colder climates should opt for a heater to blow warm air throughout the area. Either way, make sure the pipes and tubing below the floor never get cold enough to freeze. Frozen pipes can easily burst causing a huge mess and the need for expensive repairs. Pipes, hosing, and tubing are also susceptible to normal wear and tear and need to be replaced over time. The tubing should also not be left out in the extreme cold or heat for extended periods of time as this will lead to damage. Before buying, check out all the exterior hoses and tubing and make sure it is of working condition and undamaged.

Next, peer under the RV to see if there is any underbelly covering that is missing or damaged. This step will only be necessary if the potential RV is so equipped. Look for damage to the frame or chassis, damage to the holding tanks, gas fitting, gas lines, and sewer drain pipes. Dangling wires or hoses and pipes that are not properly secured are a major issue that will need immediate attention and repair. These can easily become snagged or torn off while driving potentially doing harm to the usability of the unit or permanent damage to anything that those pipes or wires supports. For instance, if the generator pipe is not working properly noxious fumes can build up in the storage bays and enter the coach leading to a buildup of gasses and potentially causing sickness for everyone inside. Additionally, leaking pipes can damage the access points to the water tanks making them not fill or empty properly, or spill during the process. If the black water pipes have been damaged, these problems can cause disgusting spills.

Next, spend some time checking the tires. Is the thread still useable? Are there any bulges in the tires? Cracks that are fairly deep or uneven wear? Tires should commonly be replaced if more than five years old. Look at the "tire code" on the tire to check the age by manufacturer date. Search the Internet for "how to read tire code dates" for more detailed information.

Asking the salespeople for their opinion of a particular product or a condition of one on the lot is fine as a source of information, but don't let them make the final decision. Along these lines, it's wise to find an excellent and trusted mechanic (who will not charge extravagantly) to check over a vehicle and discuss any problems that it may have. They can let buyers know before they make a mistake and if this happens, they are worth every penny the buyers pay. Even for those RVs in great condition, it's still nice to have them checked out to have peace of mind while traveling down the road.

Buying a used popup trailer is much simpler than a motorcoach or fifth wheel. First, open up the trailer fully, checking all hinges and hardware while doing so. Make certain everything works as it should and check the fabric and netting for signs of fraying. Fabric replacement is expensive and could be the reason the seller will let the RV "go for cheap". It's still prudent to have a mechanic check the axles, wheels, and brakes. Put soapy water on all gas line fittings. Then open the valves to let the gas flow freely and look for bubbles around the outside of the fittings. If any are found this likely indicates a leak. If any are found, ask the seller to replace any leaky gas fittings and turnover proof of this repair at the time of purchase. Any leaking gas can be especially dangerous to individuals and pets aboard so this needs to be fixed as soon as it is found!

Check inside for signs of water leaks and/or mildew. Smell the cupboards, mattresses and cushions. Look underneath the carpet if it is removable and around the corners for signs of wear or fraying. If buying a popup, check any tent type pull outs. Is the tent fabric without any tears, clean from mold, and in good leak proof shape? Are the pullouts mattresses along the walls in good shape or are they moldy and damaged from moisture? The ceiling vents and skylights should be tight when closed and the seals free from any leakage or damage from temperature extremes. If there is damage around the openings, luckily, this is usually a cheap fix. Last, individuals need to make sure their truck has a towing package and can handle the weight.

Hard-side trailers perform much better during rainstorms and other types of inclement weather and also have fewer problems after years of use. They are also able to stand up to the cold and wind much better than the soft-sided RVs which allow those inside to be more comfortable. Hard-sided units also generally require less maintenance and repair work. But on the downside, they cost more. By and large, a well-cared-for hard-sided trailer will still be as good as a new even after decades of enjoyment.

New, lightweight construction materials such as alloys and aluminum are being used more than ever before in towables. These materials allow RVs to be easily pulled by more smaller vehicles than ever before. Most often a common bumper mounted hitch is used to hook up the tow vehicle to the trailer, often with weight distribution hitches. Some of the newer models even come equipped with anti-sway features. Generally the larger and heavier the trailer, the more tow vehicle the owners will need to assure a safe towing experience. This can have an impact on the axels so assure they are in proper working order at the time of purchase.

When buying a towable, always check that that the tow vehicle will be able the handle the size and weight of the RV being towed. Many salesmen will tell any buyer who will listen that their products are the best on the market and will work for any purpose they desire. After buying a RV too many folks find out that it is simply too heavy, too long, or just plain wrong for the tow vehicle in one area or another. It's important to assure that the tow vehicle can safely pull the RV. Throwing caution to the wind and then finding out that the trailer is too cumbersome to tow safely might in fact put the owner, his or her family, and other people on the road in jeopardy! Every year, there are thousands of accidents that happen due to this problem alone! Sometimes salespeople are less than honest when trying to make a sale and will tell potential buyers that the RV is so light that it can be safely towed by any vehicle. This simply is not true. Always consult with the tow vehicle's manufacturer ratings or owner's manual to confirm before setting off!

The most frugal buyers almost always buy used. This is because RVs are similar to passenger cars and trucks in that they depreciate a lot in the first few years. The most satisfied RVers know how to complete basic home repair themselves. Even though everything was in working order at the time of purchase, most RVers find it extremely helpful to be proficient in handling the most basic repair work themselves. This includes pinpointing problem areas before the issue gets worse, tightening loose screws, reaffixing glue to any areas that need them (such as around cabinetry), tightening latches, replacing light bulbs, and dozens of other small things will have to be replaced and/or repaired along the journey. Repair shops are expensive and sometimes unnecessary so those who are able to complete tasks themselves will not only save money but learn more about RVing in the process! As Steve Jobs stated, "time is limited so do not waste it living life for someone else."

BUDGETING & FINANCING

Arranging financing is one of the most important considerations when purchasing a recreational vehicle. Loans are available from a multitude of available sources such as community credit unions, banks, to an array of financial institutions. There is no shortage of institutions willing to underwrite RV loans. Plus, there are many reputable financing sites online and there are a host of resources to guide individuals through the process.

RV loan rates are usually tied to automobile interest rates, so when auto loans are low and reasonable, RV loan rates should follow suit. For those with good credit, it will be relatively easy to negotiate competitive rates with the dealership, bank, or financial institution. RV loans are available from all those arenas, but there are specific RV financiers that specialize in motorhome and other recreational vehicle loans. Most of the time dealerships will be able to tap into those resources, quickly comparing rates and offering the most competitive terms. Largely their offers will be more financially advantageous than banks, financial institutions, or private party sales. This is because they have access to dozens of lenders with which they have an ongoing relationship and they want to sell as many RVs as possible.

Before signing with any specialty lender, make sure they have a good reputation and have been vetted by the Better Business Bureau and are in good standing. Never fill out an online loan application or send personal financial information via the Internet until verifying the creditability of the lender. Most specialty lenders will be happy to discuss information like RV loan rates and terms over the phone or by email as well. Lenders that have a strong presence online make qualifying easy and will be able to give an approval almost instantly. This will be a great help in letting potential buyers know how much they are able to afford before visiting the dealership.

RV financing can go as high as $250,000 for 20 years without an income check for those that have good to excellent credit. Used RVs are able to be financed as well, so buyers do not always have to buy a brand new motorhome to qualify for good RV financing. However, for RVs that are older than five years, potential buyers should note that these are much harder to finance as lenders to not to take the larger risk of having to resell the unit if a buyer defaults. This is because older RVs have less resale potential due to a smaller market for older units. For those who have questions about RV financing, they may simply call an RV financing company and find out just what services they offer. Applicants are usually surprised at the plethora of results!

Because motorhomes are considered for mortgages, a 15-year loan is the best way for many buyers. However, keep in mind not all RVs are acceptable for the mortgage deduction in the eyes of the Internal Revenue Service. The IRS has established minimum standards for an RV to be considered a second home. The RV normally must be self-contained and have permanent, fixed sleeping quarters, cooking and bathroom facilities. For example, even the smallest travel trailers with a stove and bathroom facilities, should qualify as a second home. However, setting up a cot in the back of a van will not turn the vehicle into an acceptable RV and the mortgage deduction will likely be denied, leading to a larger tax bill, and potentially penalties for not paying the tax bill on time.

Motorhomes are classified as homes, therefore the interest can be considered a tax deduction, but for those that run a business from their recreational vehicle and file tax paperwork stating so, also have the option of depreciating the unit.

Plus, those RVers can deduct qualified expenses from the conduct of business from their RV. One key test the IRS uses is if the expenses are considered ordinary and necessary for an individual's line of work. For example, those who use their RV to provide veterinary care for animals in the area or for home-bound patients who are unable to get to the office, can deduct the costs of mileage, fuel, business equipment, and medical supplies. But if patients always travel to the RV and it remains in a fixed location those expenses are probably not deductible.

Refinancing RV loans can save owners money and significantly reduce their monthly payments (something that can help just about anyone's financial situation). Of course, the amount saved depends on the amount left on a RV loan and any prepayment penalties which may exist. However, taking these into account, refinancing RV loans can often make a significant difference in the monthly payments. It can also save quite a bit on interest payments. When refinancing RV loans, typically owners will pay off the current loan, and then refinance a new loan with a lower balance and interest rate.

To check out refinancing an individual RV loans, visit local credit unions and banks, or look for a RV lender online. These places are great resources and will be happy to share more information about what types of loans are available and their current financing terms. They will explain who qualifies for refinancing and what the current interest rates are. If a RV was purchased several years ago and are paying a high rate of interest on the loan, refinancing just makes good financial sense. If un sure about the best deal, check with a certified tax professional or financial adviser for the best up-to-date advice on refinancing and what it can mean for an individual's financial future. There are literally thousands of banks and financial institutions that offer RV loans or have a broker or correspondent relationship with another institution that does. Be sure to vet the reputation of the financier as well as the terms before signing. When dealing with a loan broker, realize that they often sell loans to other institutions for servicing so individuals will be sending checks to different organizations throughout the life of their loan.

Alternatively, one good way to get the funds to purchase an RV is through a home equity loan from a local bank, credit union, or other financial institution. Home equity loans are usually tax deductible which saves individuals a lot of money over the life of their loan. A CPA or other tax professional will be able to provide details for individual circumstances.

Remember that a recreational vehicle will likely qualify as a home and thus, the mortgage deduction will apply. Check with a tax adviser or lawyer for all the possible deductions allowed by law. Depending on the owners' income, loan interest rate, total purchase price, and any fees, the deduction may be significant.

Financing an RV is a lot like financing a car or home. Decent credit is needed and a verifiable source of income to repay the loan. Therefore most savvy shoppers obtain a financial prequalification letter before shopping to know how much they can spend and what the loan will end up costing them. The monthly figure as well as how much they will spend over the life of the loan is important in determining the specific RVs that are available to individual buyers. Discuss interest rates for financing with a bank or credit union before visiting a dealership or RV show with the intention of buying. That way, buyers will be familiar with RV financing rates and they will be able to better negotiate financing with the dealer sales person or lending professional. Because the RV is considered a second home, the IRS allows owners to deduct the interest on the loan.

The most competitive lenders such as USAA and some credit unions will offer up to 100% financing and refinancing for customers with which they've had an ongoing relationship. These are typically only available to those with great credit and a history of strong, verifiable income. The larger the loan to value (LTV) typically, the more secure the loan needs to be for the financing company. This is because the financial institution needs to be easily able to sell the RV if a default occurs. Because of this, higher LTV loans are much more common for vehicles under one hundred thousand dollars in value. However, with exceptional credit and a high verifiable income to the overall loan amount, occasionally these requirements are waved.

Financing an RV is a lot like funding a house purchase. Most RVs will qualify for IRS tax breaks as second vacation homes, and owners can finance them for up to 20 years in many cases. There are also many companies that specialize in financing RVs or other recreational vehicles. Some even offer special features like a deduction off the monthly payment for those who set up automatic withdrawals from their checking, investment, or savings account. Some even offer financing directly through a local dealer or for particular geographic regions. This is because some banks and financial institutions mist loan a certain percentage of their total loans known as their "books" to a specific region as specified in their charter. This can be very beneficial for those looking for loans in a particular area that falls into a certain loan category.

Before signing on the dotted line and buying new RV, run the numbers through an RV financing calculator to make sure that the purchase is financially practical. Many of these calculators are available online, and it's a simple matter to put in the approximate purchase price, interest rate, and time period of the loan to find out what the payments will be. Most RV financing companies as well as banks and credit unions offer a financial calculator on their websites so potential buyers can easily figure out their payments and other loan terms online and assuring that they're affordable before signing.

RV loan rates are generally higher than home loans, but often lower than auto loans. Shop around for financing before making a purchase. For those that belong to a credit union, they often finance used as well as new RVs and the rates are among the most competitive. Financing arranged through a dealership can sometimes come with a higher annual percentage rate. Thus, a larger percentage of buyers may be qualified because there are more lenders with which the dealership is able to place these loans. But, this varies widely by jurisdiction and no two areas or dealerships will offer the exact same loan programs.

For those in the market for a used motorhome or other type of recreational vehicle, fall and early winter can be a good time to buy. While many snowbirds are heading south in their RVs in search of warmer weather, there are plenty of other folks who have enjoyed the summer camping season and are now looking to unload their rigs. This is opposed to spending time and money to store and maintain them during the long winter ahead.

Remember, RV financing loans can extend up to a structure of 20 years, depending on a borrowers balance and credit, so financing an RV might not be as costly as individuals initially may think. Buyers should complete as much research as possible and run the figures with an RV financing calculator so they are aware of the best deals before purchasing that dream RV. That will guarantee years of happiness and enjoyment as buyers get the most out of their new home on wheels!

Those who have financing ready or their checkbooks handy often score the best deals. Cash is king, but for those who need to finance, sometimes RV dealers even have the ability to secure better finance rate than banks or credit unions due to the sheer number of lending institutions with which they have an affiliation. The majority of new, non-custom recreational vehicles sell for negotiated prices of between 20 and 30 percent less than the manufacturer suggested retail price.

There are many factors that contribute to the budget of the RV owner.

Maintenance – The larger, older, and more complex a particular RV, the more things that can go wrong! A motorhome will ultimately require more maintenance than the average car or truck. Unless the buyer is extremely adept at automotive repair then this can be a considerable expense over time.

Insurance – The more expensive the RV the more likely there will be a larger insurance payment. Owners will find that insurance will be more expensive than for a typical car or truck. Insurance premiums are commensurate with the market value of that which is insured coupled with the chance that something will go wrong over the length of the policy. Unfortunately, motorhomes are complex, expensive, and ultimately more prone to have problems than most other types of transport.

Fuel/Oil - The RV marketplace is still waiting for a viable hybrid motorhome. Until then, expect to derive a fuel economy between six and 22 miles per gallon depending on the total weight and aerodynamics of the rig.

If the owner will be towing a boast, another motorhome, or secondary vehicle behind their RV they will need to consider if they have the right vehicle and equipment to do so and take into account the degradation in fuel mileage.

Towing – For most RVers, the biggest expense, once they have bought the rig of their dreams, is either the tow vehicle or the small vehicle to be towed, called a toad. With a trailer of any size, most RVers opt for at least a ¾ ton truck with a special towing package and heavy-duty suspension. For those choosing a motorhome, most feel they need to tow a small vehicle to get around after setting up camp. Anything larger than a class B or truck camper is quite impractical for driving into town for an evening out, a gallon of milk, or sightseeing. Additionally, most of the time RVers need to have the rig stay as level as possible so the refrigerator and freezer to run properly. This way their frozen foods will not thaw out and the refrigerated foods won't spoil. Parking in cities is often difficult under the best of circumstances and level sports are even more few and far between. All the more of a reason to have a toad whenever traveling.

Parking Availability – Many homeowners associations (HOAs) do not allow motorhomes to be parked within the community where owners live. Or, there simply is no space to park them. Consequently, there may be additional storage fees on top of RV payments.

Ancillary Charges – Owners often take their RV to areas or campgrounds or parks that charge an entrance fee, additional costs, or outright rent for the length of time parked. These often quickly add up and may be considerable over time.

Food & Beverages – Will the owners be preparing their own meals on board or will everyone be eating out every night? Frequently dining at restaurants, even if it is fast food, is much more expensive than grocery shopping.

Connectivity – Mobile Internet, wireless devices (such as cell phones and tablets), GPS, satellite TV, movie rental, streaming video fees, and much more all take their toll on finances. Those who are interested in having all of these services on the road will find that it is much more expensive than in a fixed location. It is also more difficult to secure a cellular signal in many unpopulated areas. Thus, a cellular strengthener or Wi-Fi booster, and a satellite auto-locater are necessities for many who are constantly traveling. Many folks rely on these communication networks for their businesses or other income and would be much less well off financially without access. These devices are an additional expense and can use a lot of electricity. This means the generator needs to be run more often or more batteries and solar cells need to be purchased to provide power.

INSURANCE & WARRANTIES

Before agreeing to purchase a motorhome make sure and thoroughly try every feature and function on the coach prior to leaving the dealer lot. Even if the dealer offers a money back guarantee or a trail period, this is still an integral step. This is because dealers know that once a motorhome leaves their lot, it is much less likely to return because buyers do not want to deal with the hassles of the return process.

Question the dealer about how they interact with the manufacturer regarding warranty issues. Make sure they detail the process, any tips for speeding up the requisite steps, as well as other pertinent information that folks need to know before submitting a claim. At a minimum, if there is a problem, definitely document every small item in detail and be ready to discuss with the claims representative.

Prior to setting off on the first road trip, consider enrolling in a roadside assistance program offered by AAA, Good Sam Club, and others to cover towing and other service expenses. The programs are easily affordable and provide some peace of mind while heading down the road in a RV. Many RVs also feel much more comfortable when they have insurance for their entire coach.

Some manufacturers limit their liability to specific parts and may not want to deal with chassis issues, or other more complicated and expensive systems. So, be careful that the manufacturer does not just cover the physical parts that they actually build such as the furniture, roof, and walls. If the manufacturer does not cover it directly, the dealer should warranty these potential issues for a limited amount of time to complete the sale. Buyers should not hesitate to ask for this concession, even if it is not offered since it's easy to make small amendments to a contract.

RVers may easily protect their investment with extended service contracts. Sometimes the RV dealership will offer extended warranties that are tailored in particular ways at different price points that begin when the factory warranty expires. When purchasing an RV, consider some other factors that will help protect this significant investment. Many RVers recommend looking into some type of extended service contract that goes beyond the manufacturer warranty period.

Additionally, there are numerous insurance plans available that cover breakdowns, repair costs, and much more. Shopping around for the best deal will lead to significant savings but make sure to only buy coverage that is needed. Coverage above and beyond what is necessary only leads to increased costs. Some RVers really enjoy their specialized RV insurance coverage which is different from home owners and automobile policies. When something goes awry and specialized coverage is needed, buyers are usually glad they have it to fall back upon.

It's up to the buyer to decide if they are willing to pay for an extended warranty. Most of the time, there is a significant profit built into these warranties and some are not worth it over the long-haul for the buyer. Many times the fine print notes many exclusions and excepted items. These warranties typically do not cover all of the items the buyers expect them too! So, read through any warranty agreement before committing. Up to 2/3rds of most aftermarket warranties end up being pure profit for the seller of the plan. So, caveat emptor!

Check with multiple insurance agents about coverage availability and cost. It would be such a shame to buy a nice RV and then discover the increased insurance premiums break the buyers' budget!

For those who live in California, (as well a few other states and municipalities) there are special requirements for larger RV owners. If the vehicle weighs greater than 26,000 lbs. or has a long wheel base (such as a bus conversion), they need a class B operator's drivers license. Sometimes these specialty licenses are more expensive and have additional training requirements prior to issuance. Potential RV owners should check with their state Department of Motor Vehicles to determine if the rig they are thinking of purchasing has any special requirements when traveling down the road.

Many folks feel that they receive the most quality for their money when buying a used RV with low mileage and some warranty coverage still available. There are many companies offer extended warranties and service contracts before, during, and after the sale. One very important thing to remember while purchasing from a dealer is that "if it isn't in writing, it didn't happen". Often times while walking around the RV sales lot, a less scrupulous salesperson will tell prospective buyers whatever they want to hear and show them whatever they can simply to secure the deal and make a commission. Later, when the buyer reads through the paperwork they find out what the salesperson said simply is not true. Always thoroughly read through all agreements before signing.

Motorhomes should not be insured with just any company. Check around while comparing prices and terms. For those who have a clean driving record, good credit, and own a fix dwelling may qualify for multiple discounts on top of better terms.

Insurance plans should make RVing easier, not lead to additional stress. So, buyers should only acquire a plan that leads to peace of mind. When RVer should remember that, to paraphrase Roy M. Goodman, "happiness is a way of traveling, not a destination."

For many there is no better way to travel from one place to another enjoying oneself the whole way. RVing connects the traveler not just with the destination, but with the journey itself!

www.ingramcontent.com/pod-product-compliance
Lightning Source LLC
Chambersburg PA
CBHW080433290526
45791CB00008BA/2485